SAINT FRANCIS OF ASSISI

Saint Francis of Assisi

(1182 - 1226)

By Msgr. Leon Cristiani

Translated from the French
by M. Angeline Bouchard

St. Paul Editions

Imprimatur:
✛ Humberto Cardinal Medeiros
    Archbishop of Boston

Original French title: "Saint François d'Assise"

NIHIL OBSTAT   IMPRIMATUR
Irénée Noye, P.S.S.   Pierre Girard, S.S., V.G.

Library of Congress Catalog Card Number: 74-79802

Printed in the U.S.A., by the Daughters of St. Paul
50 St. Paul's Ave., Boston, MA 02130

The Daughters of St. Paul are an international congregation of women religious serving the Church with the communications media.

This translation
is lovingly dedicated to
my godchildren, Francis,
Dorothy, Sheila, Michael,
and Tanya

Contents

INTRODUCTION

In the spring of 1903, a group of theological students at the French Seminary in Rome had come, as was their custom, to spend the better part of their Easter vacation at Assisi. I had been ordained to the priesthood just one year at the time, and was making my first pilgrimage to the home of that great lover of poverty, St. Francis.

We were staying at the Hotel Subiaso, where we ate our meals each day at a long table with the other guests. These included a quiet and rather austere couple, who would always sit at the end of the table, a little apart from the others. The man was about forty-five and his wife a bit younger; both were of medium height. They did not speak much, and their two half-grown children sat between them, admirably disciplined and silent. Obviously this small family group considered the hotel their home, whereas we were only transients.

We soon learned that the stern and distinguished gentleman with whom we shared our meals was none other than the great scholar and historian, Paul Sabatier.

It was also alleged he had come to Assisi with the intention of snatching Francis of Assisi from the Catholic Church, and restoring him to humanity as a whole.

I must admit that this notion, which now seems pretentious and rather ridiculous, filled me with indignation. At that time a new way of thinking, that would soon be called *Modernism*, was bursting onto the religious scene. A few of our seminary colleagues seemed to admire Paul Sabatier's plan and took every opportunity to play up to him. The whole subject led to a rather serious dispute among us.

These distant memories come to mind as I begin to write a biography of St. Francis. I feel I owe Paul Sabatier the respect he deserves. We must say that his learned research inspired a renewal of Franciscan studies.

After being a Protestant minister in two French parishes, St. Nicholas in Strasbourg, then Saint-Clergé La Serre, he had devoted himself to the study of Franciscan history. When I saw him in Assisi in 1903, he had already published a number of works, the most important being the following: *Vie de saint François d'Assise* (1894); *Un nouveau chapitre de la Vie de saint François d'Assise* (1896); Brother Leo's *Speculum perfectionis* (1898); Brother Bartholi's *Tractatus de Indulgentiis; Regula antiqua fratrum et sororum de poenitentia* (1901); *Description du Speculum vitae beati Francisci et sociorum ejus* (1903). He would continue working along these lines until his death in Strasbourg in 1928.

It would seem that the person who derived greatest profit from all these works, even while discreetly and effectively criticizing the tendencies and conclusions of Paul Sabatier, was Jens Johannes Jörgensen. This famous Danish convert died in May, 1956, at the age of ninety. He too spent long years in Assisi, which became his adopted city, and made St. Francis the sole object of his research, his meditations, and his writings. The first edition of his book, *St. Francis of Assisi*, appeared in 1909.

Jörgensen had been a novelist before his conversion to Catholicism in 1896. He brought to his new work a wonderful power of description and a captivating style, which he combined with a rigorous sense of historical accuracy.

My little book cannot compete with the works of such famous predecessors. There is one thing, however, that I have in common with both these authors and that I hope will come through to my readers. It is the deep love with which I approach my subject, that is, my keen admiration for the saint whose fruitful life I am going to tell, and whose humble son I am, in a sense, as a Franciscan Tertiary.

Paul Sabatier loved Francis because he saw in him one of the men who imitated Jesus Christ most fervently in all of history.

Johannes Jörgensen, and the many biographers who have followed him, had no trouble demonstrating the deep Catholicity of St. Francis, his love for the Church, his respect for priests, his obedience to the Pope, his veneration for the Catholic sacraments. In short, they showed that Francis of Assisi was as Catholic as St. Louis, King of France, who was a Franciscan Tertiary; as Joan of Arc; Teresa of Avila; Thérèse of Lisieux; and such Franciscan saints as Bonaventure, Bernardine of Siena, Leonard of Port Maurice, and so many others.

We propose to write history in a very modest way, without trying to prove any thesis. We shall keep as close as possible to the sources: the two biographies by Thomas de Celano, the *Fioretti*, the *Major Life of St. Francis* by St. Bonaventure, and *The Legend of the Three Companions*. We shall offer our readers facts, authentic traditions, revered texts, and nothing more.

CHILDHOOD, YOUTH, SUDDEN CONVERSION

The kiss to the leper

Did this episode occur in 1206 or 1207? That is not easy to say. But even if the exact date is uncertain, it did happen, and it had decisive consequences. Let us tell it in its simple truth.

An elegant and handsome young knight—about twenty-four or twenty-five years old—was riding his horse in the countryside near the city of Assisi. He was deep in thought and paid little attention to the beauty of the landscape which he knew so well. Suddenly his horse reared back and came to a halt. The young man looked up and saw before him a wretched man asking for alms, whose distinctive attire marked him as a leper. Leprosy was, and still is, looked upon with horror, and the young horseman was particularly terrified of leprosy. His first impulse was to turn and flee. But no! Given the thoughts he had in his heart, he could not yield to his natural fears. This leper before him was asking for a sign of charity, a gesture of love. Was not this encounter providential? In a flash the young man asked himself this question and saw the answer. Jumping down from his mount, he approached the leper, who was holding his hand out, took a princely alms from his purse and placed it in the fingers gnawed by leprosy and covered with wounds and ulcers.

But was it enough to give an alms, to throw a gold piece to a miserable leper? Had his heart guessed who this man really was? Christ had said: "As often as you did it for one of my least brothers, you did it for me" (Mt. 25:40). Was Christ satisfied with the young knight's commonplace act? Certainly not. More was required. There was call for a personal witness, a proof of friendship. Without cogitating as long as we have here, Francis—for that was the young knight's name—bent down quickly and kissed the horrible hand of the poor leper, who looked up with joyful surprise.

Twenty years later when Francis was preparing his last will and *Testament* shortly before he died, he wrote: "The Lord first demanded of me, Brother Francis, to do penance in this way. When I was still living in my sins, I experienced strong revulsion at the sight of lepers. Now the Lord Himself led me to them, and I showed compassion for them. And when I went away from them, what had formerly been bitter to me was changed into sweetness, both for my soul and my senses. And very soon afterwards I abandoned the life of the world."

There can be no doubt about it. The kiss given to the leper in 1206 or 1207 was a turning point. Besides, after his first experience Francis went—this time purposefully and not by chance—to the leper hospital at the gates of Assisi. When he arrived there, he was allowed to enter because it appeared he was bringing alms. From every part of the hospital the sick came running, their faces and limbs eaten with leprosy and their bodies giving off an infernal odor. Francis was probably suffocated at first, but by an heroic effort of will he triumphed over his revulsion and distributed the alms from his well-filled purse. As he did this, he deposited a tender kiss on each of the hands extended to receive alms.

He had just won a brilliant victory over his natural instincts, over his innate fastidiousness, over the selfishness that is so natural to man. This was to be the wellspring of all the graces God had in store for him.

But how had this handsome young man, in the glow of vitality and success, come to this?

To find out, we must look at his childhood and youth.

Birth, education

Francis was born in the month of September, probably in the year 1182, although some claim it was in 1181. He was immediately baptized and given the name of *Giovanni*, or John, in the city's cathedral, dedicated to St. Rufinus. His father, a prosperous cloth merchant, was known as *Bernardone*, "big Bernard," but the family name was Moriconi.

It seems the family came from Lucca, but Bernardone had come with his young wife, Pica, to Assisi, an ancient city of Umbria, to carry on his thriving business. We have reason to believe he often had to travel in connection with his work. He was even absent from home when his oldest son was born.

When he returned, he decided that the boy would be called *Francesco*. Perhaps he was just back from a journey to France where he had had successful business dealings. The name Francesco actually means "Frenchman." In any event, Francis was to keep the name his father chose for him. And he became so famous that in future generations literally countless numbers of little Christians were to be called Francis in his honor. It is certain that the boy learned to speak French as a small child, and later loved to sing in French because he found its musical sounds particularly pleasing.

The young Francis was educated like the other more privileged children of his time. His father moved among the wealthy and powerful of his city. Money was never lacking in the Bernardone household, and at that period of history money was beginning once again to be a means to social prestige. The oldest son of the rich Bernardone was naturally treated with favor at school.

The school was very close to Francis' home. It was run by the priests of the church of St. George, located on the spot where the church of St. Clare now stands.

Francis learned to read and write like the other boys of the city. The reader used in school was probably, there as elsewhere, the Latin Psalter. In those days the rod played a large role in education. Even St. Louis, King of France, was beaten by his tutor when he misbehaved. We should not be surprised if Francis was sternly chastised at school, for it was the universal custom. Besides, we know that Francis was turbulent and lively, always ready to take part in pranks as well as games. How far did he go in his studies? It is hard to say. He later claimed he was "illiterate," meaning that he had not pursued any advanced studies. We should note that universities had not yet come into existence in his time. One of the most serious problems he was to face as the founder of a religious order was how to provide his sons with higher education, and this problem would cause him great anxiety.

However, Francis certainly learned enough Latin to understand the liturgical texts, and we know he constantly consulted his missal to discover signs of God's will for himself and his followers.

Golden youth

It must be said that while Francis was never a scholar, never a great theologian or brilliant scholastic philosopher, he gave evidence of superior intellectual gifts throughout his life. He was a poet in the deepest and most beautiful sense of the word, that is to say, an *inspired* man, a *creator*. And this is the primary sense of the word *poet*. To his eyes everything took on symbolic meaning. His mind could discern God and the infinite in all things. Isn't that the truest kind of intelligence?

Besides, being of a naturally cheerful disposition he was, without knowing it, intoxicated with life. He had songs to sing for every hour and every occasion. When he could not think of a song he had learned, he would invent one. Everything we know of his adolescence indicates that he drew others by his outgoing personality. He quite naturally became the center, the leader of his group, the life of any and all festivities he attended. He never sulked. The world smiled upon him and he smiled in return. That's what we mean by his "golden youth."

We should note that as a young man he was strongly attracted to tales of chivalry. The tastes of this merchant's son were definitely not those of a shopkeeper. While he faithfully did his job in his father's store, he lost no opportunity to spend every cent he had earned and whatever else besides his mother gave him. She was probably more lenient than his father, who was often away on business. Lady Pica was so proud of Francis! He was such a cheerful, courteous, loving, and gracious son, with the gift of making others love him. So she yielded to his every whim. But his whims were never commonplace or vulgar. We read in the earliest biography, *The Three Companions,* attributed to his first three disciples:

"He had such a desire to make people laugh and to be popular that he once had a garment made of very expensive cloth sewn to some very cheap goods."

This means he sometimes dressed as a juggler like the traveling minstrels of the time. And he probably went out the way they did, to sing popular songs of chivalry.

We also know, beyond doubt, that in his convivial activities, in his songs and amusing disguises, there was never anything improper, suspect, vulgar, or sordid. He was always a lover of good manners and propriety. Nor do we find any trace of light lovemaking in his "golden youth." He was especially fond of banquets, and he was usually the one who treated his comrades. But while they drank good wine, ate succulent food, and sang many songs at the gatherings he hosted, nothing was done that could offend Christian sensibilities.

Such restraint could spring only from a deep and authentic piety. He could never have reached the heights of pure love later on, had he not been nourished from childhood with an abundant love, a love that would grow into the impetuous torrent we have yet to describe. But these are conjectures on our part. What we do know is that a day came when his frothy, carefree adolescence was matured by trials and suffering. Then his underlying piety came to his aid to help him understand the vanity of all things. Indeed his past amusements would then seem like so

many sins, or at least as time snatched from true
love. Then only would a reformed, mature Francis,
transformed and sustained by divine grace, attain
his identity, and become one of the greatest lovers of
the cross of Christ who ever lived.

Certainly his later spiritual development can
be explained only in the light of his deep-seated piety.
But to this we must also add his charity toward the
poor. As we have pointed out, he understood very
early Jesus' words: "As often as you did it for one of
my least brothers, you did it for me" (Mt. 25:40).
He also knew that according to the Gospel we must
give not only to those who can requite us, but by
preference to those who cannot.

One day when, contrary to his custom, he had
thoughtlessly turned away a beggar without giving
him alms, he was immediately filled with remorse.
His earliest biographers tell us he was greatly ashamed
of this lack of charity, and said "he would surely
have given if this man had come to him on behalf
of one of his noble friends, but he should have
remembered that he came to him on behalf of the
King of kings, the Master of masters!" St. Bonaventure, who reports the incident, adds that he ran after
the beggar as fast as he could and gave him the alms
he had at first refused. He must certainly have added
some kind words to heal the wound his earlier refusal
had caused.

Traits such as this reveal his essential character
even in early life. There would be need of many
improvements in his total personality, but already
people could say of Francis what had been said of
John the Baptizer: "What do you think this young man
will become?" Sometimes this question was asked
of his mother, pointing out that her son was quite a
spendthrift. On one occasion she answered very
gently: "I have the hope that some day he, too, will
become a child of God."

Lady Pica must have accompanied this prophecy with many maternal prayers. But she had no idea her words were so true.

The hour soon came when God laid His hand on Francis and knotted the thread of his destiny so tightly that it would never break.

In prison

It is usually through the events of life that God manifests His will and gives us an opportunity to manifest ours. Human history is made up of these external events. The deeper history that God writes in us is made up of our responses to events. Francis was born and lived in a time and place troubled by conflict. In Assisi, the burghers and lower classes had risen against certain of the nobles. These nobles, for their part, sought help from the neighboring city of Perugia. The details of the quarrel are of little importance to us now. We need only remember that a war broke out between Assisi and Perugia. The forces from Assisi were roundly beaten near St. John's Bridge on the plain between the two towns, and Francis, an apprentice knight (although a merchant's son), was taken prisoner.

The Battle of St. John's Bridge was fought in 1202, when Francis was twenty years old. He and the other prisoners were crowded into a filthy building and treated with the harshness common at that time. And their captivity lasted a whole year. To be forced at the age of twenty to remain in a cell for twelve months, to suffer privations and cruel treatment, as well as humiliation, is enough to dishearten ordinary men. And this is precisely what happened to most of the prisoners of Perugia, with a single exception. We have the most reliable evidence on this point.

Francis raised the morale of all his fellow prisoners. He still had songs to sing and cheerful things to say despite their troubles. And where did he draw this interior peace? In later years, a Napoleon Bonaparte would speak of his "star." Francis had a higher assurance. He knew that God was with him, that some day God would take him by the hand and he would only have to follow. As we have said, the thread was knotted around his destiny, and he knew it. When others seemed surprised at his cheerfulness in their sad circumstances, he would answer brightly but with deep conviction: "Do you not know that I have a great future to look forward to, and that the whole world will some day bow before me and pay me homage?"

What did he mean? Each of us has a right to say, as he thinks about his immortal soul: "I have a great future to look forward to." But as for adding: "People will bow before me and pay me homage!" That was just a daydream of Francis' poetic soul. And although he didn't know it, his daydream was in a great part prophetic.

In November, 1203, peace was signed between Perugia and Assisi, under acceptable conditions. The prisoners were returned, and Francis came home. But despite the unfortunate campaign of 1202, he was more than ever enamored of chivalric adventures and the merry science of the troubadours.

Strangely enough, the trial he had just been through had partly disillusioned him, without however opening up any new vistas. He was troubled and sensed the emptiness of his life; he prayed God to enlighten him, but did not yet receive any answer from heaven. There is a moment for everything in the plans of Providence. Francis' hour would come a little later. Meanwhile, he still had the ambition to become in truth the knight he was still in desire only.

With Walter de Brienne

About this time there was talk in Assisi about a certain "gentleman," whose name is absent from the earliest biographies of Francis, but whom we identify as Gauthier de Brienne. He was the brother of the John de Brienne who was to distinguish himself later by capturing Damietta in Egypt from the Saracens. Walter de Brienne was fighting in the service of Pope Innocent III. He was to die in June, 1205, at the siege of Sarno. In Assisi, a nobleman had become an enthusiastic follower of de Brienne and set out with a small group of his fellow townsmen to join him. Francis was among them!

This would seem to confirm everything we have said about the amazing interests of this merchant's son. Decidedly, he had no taste for shop-keeping. When he enrolled in the war against Perugia, his father could applaud his determination and courage. It was perfectly in line with Bernardone's ambitions that his son march in the front line of the Assisi burghers, and go to battle like the most valiant noblemen of the city. For Bernardone dreamed of a great future for his son in Assisi. But this was something entirely different. Francis was going on a distant expedition in the service of Walter de Brienne, abandoning the family store, and joining with knights who were not of his class. For Bernardone, this looked like a utopian undertaking, an adventure he could not understand and that could not be very productive.

What was his puzzling son, so different from himself, aspiring to do? We agree with his earliest biographers in saying that he dreamed of becoming a knight. He could already picture himself as an armed knight, receiving gold spurs from the great leader in whose service he was enlisting. *The Three Companions*, the authors of one of the earliest and most reliable biographies of Francis, recount that in his excitement Francis was floating on air. He no longer walked but ran, practically flew through the streets. His habitual cheerfulness was now out of bounds. His eyes shown with joy. When anyone asked him why he was so happy, he would answer in the half-joking, half-serious tone we noticed during his captivity in Perugia: "I know that I'm going to become a great prince!"

The thread of his destiny had been firmly tied. God was pulling on the thread, and Francis felt himself being pulled. But he didn't yet see where he was going. Events were to point the way. For it is always through events that God makes His will known to us. It is up to us to know how to interpret them, and follow the path God has chosen for us.

So Francis set out on his new campaign. He had spared no expense to equip himself, for he was a rich young man. When he was finally ready to depart for foreign lands, he must have been a sensation in Assisi. He dreamed of feats of valor and winning great battles.

Then one day he was on his way. He rode his horse down the hill on which his native city is so charmingly perched, and started toward Foligno. From there he meant to go to Spoleto, and follow the ancient Flaminian Way to Rome and southern Italy.

But his journey was a short one. The hour willed by God had come to give Francis' life a new and unexpected direction.

Although we are a bit uncertain as to our saint's chronology at this time, we shall situate two events in his life either in 1204 or 1205. The first was irresistible: illness. The second, which was added to the first, was a vision, or rather what is called a "divine locution" in mystical theology.

After returning from his year's captivity in Perugia, Francis had already been sick. It was no doubt a recurrence of his illness that stopped him in Spoleto. He couldn't go any further, for he was stricken with a high fever. And as he lay on his sickbed, half-awake and half-asleep, he thought he heard a voice questioning him:

"Where do you want to go?" the voice said.

"To Apulia, to become a knight!"

"Now, tell me," the voice replied, "who is best able to serve you, the master or the servant?"

"The master!" the nonplused Francis answered.

"In that case, why are you abandoning the master for the servant, and the prince for his vassal?"

Francis had understood. Like St. Paul on the road to Damascus, he cried out:

"Lord, what do you want me to do?"

And the voice declared:

"Return to your own city. There you will be told what you must do, because what you have seen must be understood differently from the way you have understood it."

Francis then came out of a deep sleep, and tried in vain to go back to sleep.

The voice he had heard continued to haunt him. In the morning, he got up, and without worrying about the humiliation he would encounter, returned to Assisi. He had renounced forever his dream of being an armed knight, and was ready to enter, at God's call, a knighthood of an entirely different kind: the knighthood of divine love.

Rapid development

Immediately after returning from his abortive expedition Francis entered a period of rapid development. He felt he could not resume his former life. He did not have the vocation to be a merchant like his father, and whenever he worked in the family store it was without enthusiasm. The money he earned burned his fingers. He would turn around and spend it among the poor and even more often in festivities which he offered to his friends. But here too he experienced a strange disenchantment. One evening, perhaps during the summer of 1205, he gave a glittering banquet for his companions. Once again, he felt like the "king of the party," and as others said of him later, like "the flower of youth."

At the end of this joyful and noisy gathering, when the guests were going home, singing in the streets, Francis felt suddenly overcome by the emptiness of his life. He let the others go on ahead of him. He could no longer join in their songs, and soon found himself alone in one of the steep alleys of the city—alone and as though lost in a dream that was tragic yet filled with sweetness. He was almost unconscious of everything around him. As he said later on, he might have been cut up in pieces and he would never have noticed it.

However, one of his comrades came back to find him and tried to pull him out of his trance.

"Tell me, Francis," he asked, "is it the thought of a forthcoming marriage that makes you stand there like a man of stone?"

"Yes," he replied, "I am seriously thinking of getting married, and the bride I have chosen is the noblest, richest, and most beautiful of all the women you know!"

Meanwhile his other friends had gathered around. The fine dinner had filled them with good cheer, and they said laughingly:

"In that case, your tailor is going to be very busy again. It will be even worse than when you were leaving for Apulia!"

These words, these peals of laughter, completely upset Francis and destroyed all the joy he had had in his past pleasures.

The Three Companions declared quite clearly: "From that very hour, he began to despise himself."

These are deep words which indicate that a radical change had come about in his soul. His heart had been touched by a new grace. It was the hour when, like Augustine before him, he cried within his soul: "How much longer?" Everything seemed insipid to him. Everything seemed vain except the love of Jesus and His cross. He was no longer—he would never again be—the easygoing and presumptuous young man he had been, the merry comrade who took everything with a laugh and a song, the aspiring knight who wanted to parade on a beautiful horse in magnificent attire. He was on the march. He didn't know where he was going. But the thread that God was pulling led him further and further. In the next chapter we shall see what happened to our Francis. The ordinary way of life had lost its appeal for him. He was starting a new life. But he didn't want it to be empty like the one he had been living. To begin with, he would fill his life with God.

BUILDER OF CHURCHES

The prayer of expectation

When we think of the plans God had for Francis, we admire the infinite art with which He succeeded in bending him to His unknown intentions. Francis would not be a merchant like his father, nor a knight as he himself had hoped.

Of course, he could have entered one of the Orders or a monastery. Many young men before him, convinced of the greatness of the human vocation and the nothingness of the ordinary way of life among men, had left the world to become monks or priests. In the preceding century, Norbert, also a kind of "prince of youth," had heard the divine call and founded the new Order of the Premonstratensians.

At the same period, Bernard, who was equally outstanding among the young noblemen of France, had pleaded so well the cause of a life totally hidden in God that he had led thirty of his companions to the solitude of Citeaux, and later would found the Abbey of Clairvaux.

Francis belonged to the same spiritual family as Norbert and Bernard. God was going to call him to a mission analogous to theirs. But God's ways are beyond counting. There are not two flowers exactly alike. Divine wisdom has infinite resources.

The first fruit of this transformation, as Francis experienced it, was a great attraction to prayer. He realized that only God could fill the emptiness he had sensed in his life. In describing this change in him, St. Antoninus of Florence said: "Sometimes he would remain in solitary caves, and at other times he would work devoutly to rebuild churches."

But above all else, he prayed. He remained for hours, even days, talking intimately with God in a solitary cave not far from Assisi. Of all the friends he had once had, only one stood by and sometimes went to pray with him. We do not even know this friend's name.

What did Francis say to God in his long talks with Him? Obviously, he must have said what any man in similar circumstances would say, what the high priest Heli had counseled Samuel to say: "*Speak, Lord, for your servant is listening*" (1 Sm. 3:9). It was a prayer of expectation. "Lord, what do You want me to do?"—"What is the noblest use I can put my life to?" These are the anguished questions a soul of fire formulates in such circumstances. And Francis certainly must have looked back on his youth and deplored its mistakes. Although to most people his life must have seemed full of happiness and *joie de vivre,* he saw it as a lamentable series of infidelities, shabby actions, absurd ambitions, a life of commonplace and vulgar pleasures.

God did not answer his supplications at once, although He was certainly at work within him. The disgust, regrets, and remorse, the desires for a new life, the prolonged prayers and acts of repentance came to him from God. St. Paul, St. Augustine, and all the theologians of grace would assure us of it. But these feelings poured so freely from Francis' soul that he could well have thought everything came from within him and God was not really speaking at all. This silence of God was a torture, an expiation, but also—though he didn't know it—a preparation. As *The Three Companions* has said, he found pleasure only in prayer. He experienced "a kind of compulsion that would throw him into prayer in the street, among other people, in fact, wherever he was." We learn from the same text that he would give the poor everything he had, even his clothes; or he would give to deprived churches, which was the first manifestation of a type of charity he would practice throughout his life.

Pilgrimage to Rome

About this time he made his first pilgrimage to Rome, probably early in 1206.

There is something we must point out here. Francis openly gave up his father's business. The latter would soon react strongly against the whims of his eldest son, and a complete rupture would occur between them in the bishop's presence. However, our sources do not give us any details about these events. We have to make up for their silence by conjectures of our own.

The following facts can be accepted as quite certain: First, Francis' father was often absent from Assisi on business, for he had to travel a great deal. We know that he went not only into Provence, but even much farther, into France (for Provence was not then a part of France), probably to the fairs of Champagne and elsewhere. Second, Francis' mother had great admiration for her son and let him do everything he wanted without making any objections, even giving him all the money he wanted for his alms and travels. Third, it seems Guido, the Bishop of Assisi, who was a devout person, was kept informed about everything that was happening in the Bernardone household, the transformation of soul Francis was experiencing, and his immense desires to serve God. For, when the decisive hour came, it was he, the bishop, who took Francis under his protection.

We must not forget these three points.

Now, let us come back to the pilgrimage to Rome. Francis arrived in Rome with a well-filled wallet. However, he didn't want to use his money to make a comfortable and luxurious pilgrimage. On the contrary, it was while he was in Rome that he first got the idea that would later fill his whole soul. He wanted to use his money for the poor, but was that enough? For someone else perhaps, but not for him. He certainly must have seen armies of beggars all around the Basilica of St. Peter. He saw them in their destitution, in their rags, in their humiliation, and a wild idea came to him. He would become one of them at least for a few hours or a few days. He would thus know from experience what it means to be poor, and perhaps, God willing, he would "marry poverty"!

Undoubtedly he did not see at the start where this would lead him. But he did not conceive this wild project without a special inspiration. It reminds us of what St. Paul had called "the folly of the cross." St. Paul had also said of Christ Jesus: "He emptied himself and took the form of a slave" (Phil. 2:8). And so Francis, the son of the rich merchant Bernardone, dreamed of "emptying himself by taking the form of a beggar." He had exchanged his clothes with the poorest of those who were begging from pilgrims at the doors of St. Peter's. Then, according to *The Three Companions,* he joined the other beggars "on the steps of the church" under the portico of the basilica.

Interestingly, one of our texts tells us that he begged for alms "in French, a language he liked to speak although he didn't know it very well." Speaking French seemed to take him out of his original milieu. He felt he was changing his life-style. Besides, he spoke French only when he was happy. He loved to sing in French. When he begged for alms in French he felt he was translating the joy he felt in being poor.

How long did this experiment last? We do not know. He seems to have shared the beggar's squalid meal. Then he returned the poor man's clothes and took back his own, gave the man all the money his begging had brought in and added a generous alms of his own. After that, he returned to Assisi.

It was then that the episode with the leper, recounted in the first chapter, probably took place. Francis, as we know, kissed a leper's hand and re-solved to overcome his revulsion to the disease by making frequent visits to the leper hospital of Assisi. As we have already mentioned, in his last will and *Testament* written at the end of his life, he con-sidered this the moment of his true conversion.

The only answer God had given to his prayers thus far was this interior response:

"Francis, all the things your senses have loved and desired, you must now scorn and hate. That is the only way you can know My will! But the moment you enter this new path, everything you formerly thought sweet and delightful will become bitter and unbearable; and in return, everything you formerly hated will be changed to sweetness and superabundant joy."

The leper's kiss was the demonstration of this divine promise. As *The Three Companions* tells us, Francis, who until then always "turned his face away and closed his nostrils" when he met a leper, had succeeded in overcoming himself. He would soon be rewarded by receiving new favors.

The hunchbacked woman

We also find the following episode in *The Three Companions,* one of our most reliable sources: "There was a hunchbacked and misshapen woman in Assisi whom the devil had brought to Francis' mind in an apparition. Then he threatened to cast this woman's infirmities on him if he didn't renounce his projects of holiness. But Francis, that valiant soldier of Christ, scorned the devil's threats and went into his cave to pray."

This account is a reminder of the violent diabolic persecutions Francis endured. We should not be surprised that Satan wanted to terrify him. He had done as much in the desert in the time of Anthony and Pachomius. That is what he ordinarily does within souls sincerely resolved to give themselves to God. As Böhme has said, "The devil is God's cook. Without him, life would be just tasteless pap." In Francis' case, the intervention of the devil added a dramatic element to his conversion. In his jousts with the devil, he was apprenticed in his new "knighthood."

The crucifix of St. Damian's

It was shortly after Francis kissed the leper that God deigned to speak to him and give his new life as a convert its first goal. The event has been situated in the year 1206, when he was twenty-four years old. It happened in a little church dedicated to St. Damian—a poor rustic chapel, whose only treasure was a large Byzantine crucifix above the main altar.

Francis had often entered this deserted church to pray at the feet of the crucified Jesus. That day he said the following prayer, which the Franciscan annalist Wadding has preserved for us:

"Great and magnificent God, my Lord Jesus Christ! I beseech You to enlighten me and to dispel the darkness from my soul! Give me an upright faith, firm hope, perfect charity! And grant me, Lord, the grace of knowing You well enough that I may act in all things according to Your light and in accordance with Your holy will!"

Once again we hear the poignant cry of the young Samuel: "Speak, Lord, for your servant is listening!"

And finally, the answer came, an answer that Francis heard deep within his soul, a clear and precise answer formulated in this way:

"Go, Francis, and rebuild My house, for it is about to fall into ruins!"

What house was this? History will answer without hesitation. The house was the Church of Christ—the divided, diminished Church, unsettled by schisms, heresies, apostasies—the Church that even the Pope, in a dream, would soon see about to crumble, held up only by the shoulder of a poor beggar who looked just like Francis!

But all this would become evident only after many years. And in his deep humility Francis was far from conceiving such great plans on his own.

He therefore very modestly took these words addressed to him in their literal sense. The "house of God about to crumble into ruins" was right there before his eyes. It was quite clearly the poor chapel of St. Damian. He would therefore set to work at once, with the joy of knowing he was doing a task commanded by God Himself! As he was leaving the chapel he noticed the old priest who served the chapel, sitting on a bench. With the greatest respect he came up to him, greeted him and gave him a gold piece to keep a vigil light burning before the crucifix, from which a voice had spoken to his heart. The text of *The Three Companions* assures us that from that moment whenever Francis thought of the sufferings of Christ on the cross, his heart was "fused" with the heart of Christ. And St. Bonaventure thinks that from that day on, Francis "bore in his soul the wounds of the Lord Jesus." We shall see how this very Franciscan sentiment of union with the cross of Christ the Savior was to grow unceasingly in Francis.

At work

Francis began by taking the work of rebuilding St. Damian's very seriously. He knew this would require a large sum of money. Without hesitating, he loaded a horse with a great quantity of cloth from his father's store and set out to sell it in Foligno. Even the horse was finally sold along with the merchandise. Francis rushed back to St. Damian's and turned all the money over to the old priest, telling him it was to rebuild the chapel. The priest was surprised and confused. Wasn't this some sort of madness? Would he not be castigated by this young prodigal's father for accepting such a sum? In his uncertainty, he simply put the money in a corner of the chapel, and would only promise Francis that he would pray to St. Damian.

Meanwhile Bernardone, back from a journey, was greatly irritated not to find his eldest son at home, and to learn, besides, that he had gone to Foligno with a horse and a large quantity of cloth. When he heard that Francis had been seen around

St. Damian's, he immediately went to the chapel. The old priest told him everything that had happened, and returned to him the money he had received from Francis to rebuild the chapel. Bernardone was appeased by the words he had just heard, and felt he had been sufficiently informed as to his son's wild schemes. He returned to Assisi in a serene mood. According to Celano, Francis was living completely "detached from the world" in a cave near St. Damian's, spending his nights and days in prayer and fasting, with unspeakable tears and sighs. He received a small amount of food from his father's house, doubtlessly sent by his mother.

Francis' first experience of his new life was an entire month's retreat early in 1207. Where was he going? He had no idea. It is remarkable, as we have already said, that he had no thought either of entering a monastery or of becoming a priest. During his long prayers he received no inspiration in those directions. For the time being, he was satisfied to pray, sigh, contemplate the suffering Christ, and live with the single thought of his Savior's passion.

It was unquestionably during this period of waiting that he happened to go into the plain below Assisi to pray at Portiuncula, a very tiny and ancient chapel dedicated to St. Mary of the Angels. A passer-by met him and found him in this state, that is, weeping bitterly. The man was touched at the sight of so much sorrow, and asked him the reason for his tears:
"I am weeping," said Francis, "over the sufferings of my Lord Jesus Christ, and I would not be ashamed to go all over the world and let everyone see the tears I am shedding here."

The passer-by was so deeply moved that he, too, began to weep. The two of them stayed there for a long while, sharing their tears.

The decisive crisis

However, nothing was yet settled. Francis
had renounced the world, but his father was still
counting on him. Sooner or later Bernardone would
try to catch up with his son, or at least get a definitive explanation from him. The circumstances
led to such an explanation during the month of
March, 1207. One day, a gang of urchins, shouting
and jeering, brought Francis back to his father's
house, pelting him with garbage and taunting him
all the way. When Bernardone saw his son in the
midst of this mocking troupe, he was very angry.
He went after the frightened boys, distributing
slaps and kicks to the more aggressive ones.

Then he grabbed Francis, dragged him through
the house down to a dark cellar, and locked the
door on him. Francis was subjected to a harsh diet
of bread and water. Bernardone must have thought
such a punishment would bear the fruit he expected,
for his son had been quite a gourmet in days past.
This hard penance should bring him to his senses.

It was all wasted effort. Francis was a changed
man. From now on, it would be a joy for him to
suffer for his Savior, *with* his Savior. And so when the
father set off on another journey, and Lady Pica
let her son out of the cellar, Francis showed no
resentment for the ill-treatment he had received.
Rather, he declared he was more resolved than
ever to live only for the Lord.

We have good reason to think that the young
man went to see his holy bishop, Guido, to ask his
advice about everything that was happening to him.
And the bishop, with due respect for God's will,
insisted on conferring the tonsure and the minor
orders upon him. Since Francis had been commanded
to "rebuild the Lord's house," he would at least
have an official title, a canonical title, to empower

him to do it. The way Francis would soon place himself under the protection of his bishop suggests that something happened in the interim that our texts have not clearly stated.

Francis would never become a priest. He did not think himself worthy of it. But he would receive the right to preach that is attached to the diaconate. Although we do not know the exact dates when Francis received the various orders below the diaconate, we must believe they were conferred upon him and that he considered himself, in a certain sense, a "man of the Church," that is to say, a *cleric*. And this will be apparent in the famous scene we shall soon relate.

Francis renounces his father

When Bernardone returned from his journey he did not find his son at home. This time, he decided to complain to the magistrates of the city and to publicly disinherit his insubordinate child. While the consuls were taken by surprise at this unusual complaint, they could not afford to insult a man as important as Bernardone by rejecting it. Besides, most of them must have judged Francis' conduct severely, thinking he was more or less mad, and deserved to be subjected to certain measures of civil interdiction. The herald of the city was sent to St. Damian's where Francis was known to be staying, and summoned him to appear. But he answered confidently:

"Through the grace of God, I have now become a free man. Therefore I do not consider myself obliged to appear before the consuls, since I have no other master but God!"

Such an answer could only be understood as an affirmation that he belonged to the Church as a member of the clergy. That is how the consuls, and then Bernardone himself, understood it. But since Francis' words were not absolutely clear, his father brought his complaint to the bishop. Bishop Guido didn't find this unusual, since he agreed to convoke the father and son before him, to settle their differences.

Then something memorable happened that would be an outstanding event in the history of the Church.

"Francis," said the bishop, "your father complains bitterly about you, and he is very angry. If you really intend to dedicate yourself to God's service, you must first return your father's money to him, for you no longer have any right to it. God does not want you to use it for the good of the Church, and by this restitution you can no doubt appease your father's anger." And the prelate added gently: "Trust in God, my son. The Lord will come to your aid and will help you to rebuild His Church."

These last words were significant. They proved that Guido was aware of everything that was going on. There was a good-sized crowd present, and everyone's eyes turned toward Francis. The young man answered very calmly, but with gleaming eyes:

"Most gladly, Lord, shall I return to my father not only all the money that is his, but also the clothes I have received from him." Going into an adjoining room, he soon returned wearing only a hair shirt and carrying his clothes in his arms.

"Listen, all of you, to what I have to say!" Francis continued. "Until now I have called Peter di Bernardone my father. Now I return his gold and the clothes I have received from him. From now on I shall no longer say: 'My father, Peter di Bernardone,' but 'Our Father who art in heaven!'"

With that, he bowed low, placed his outer garments and underclothing on the floor, piled on them whatever money he still had, then stood up motionless and serene.

Many of those present could not hold back their tears. Even the bishop did not hide his emotion. Only Bernardone remained unmoved and implacable. He took the money and clothing without saying a word, and quickly left the room. The bishop placed his own cloak around Francis and offered him asylum. Some castoff clothes that had belonged to the gardener were found for him. Bonaventure tells in his biography of the saint that Francis traced a large cross with a piece of chalk on the back of his shabby coat, and thus left the residence of the bishop, who had now become his protector.

Rebuilder

Not for a moment had Francis lost sight of the mission the crucifix at St. Damian's had suggested: to rebuild the church in ruins. During a quick trip to Gubbio, he was waylaid by some ruffians to whom he proudly said: "I am the herald of the great King!" He then returned to St. Damian's wearing sandals and a tunic with a cincture around the hips, gifts of a friend. This was to be his attire and that of his disciples. But there was no question of getting disciples now. In fact, there seemed no possibility he would ever have any.

His problem, as he saw it, was to obtain stones to rebuild the church of St. Damian, with the permission of the good chaplain, who had become his friend. He had no money, of course, since he had returned it all to his father. He had chosen to be poor, and he would remain poor. The poor have two ways of providing for their needs: they can work or they can beg. Francis was not afraid of work. On the contrary, he wanted to work as hard as he possibly could. Begging is a form of humiliation, and also an opportunity to inspire others to charity.

Francis was to use both means alternatively and at the same time.

One market day, he appeared in his hermit's habit, a long, grey, hooded tunic, and began to sing in the midst of the crowd like a troubadour of God. And when he had finished his song, he moved among his dumfounded hearers, saying: "Whoever gives me a stone will receive a reward in heaven, whoever gives me two stones will receive two, and whoever gives me three stones will receive three!"

And he explained to everyone that these stones would be used to rebuild St. Damian's. Naturally, there were some who laughed, and others who scoffed. Francis laughed with them. But, according to an early account, there were others who "were moved to tears." People remembered what Francis had been and they were amazed at what he had become. The stones began to pour in. He transported them himself to his new stone yard and set to work with a song. When anyone stopped to watch him, he would call out to the passer-by: "Come on over and help me rebuild the church of great St. Damian."

The old priest was delighted at Francis' zeal, and gave him his supper every night. But Francis soon felt ashamed of living at the old priest's expense, and asked himself: "Is this living like a poor man, as I want to do? No! A poor man begs from door to door with his bowl, and he mixes together everything the kind people are willing to give him."

This was to be a new trial, whose horrors he had not foreseen. He did indeed go from door to door with his bowl, and was given whatever was on hand. The result was a nondescript, revolting broth that turned Francis' stomach, for he had always had a very delicate appetite. But finally he got his courage up and began to eat. And the same thing happened to him now as after his first kiss to the leper. The sweetness of a new victory warmed his soul. He felt as though flooded with divine grace. And it seemed he had never eaten a more delectable meal.

From that day on, Francis told the priest of St. Damian he would be able to provide his own food.

Our ancient accounts offer us several striking episodes of that initial period. Once, Francis is said to have met his father in the street, who roundly insulted him; then one of his brothers, Angelo, mocked him unmercifully, saying to one of his friends: "Why don't you go and ask Francis to sell you two cents' worth of his sweat!"

Francis answered him *in French*, an indication that this language was often spoken in his father's house: "I'll sell that sweat to the Lord, and at a very high price!"

On another occasion, Francis was begging for oil to be used for the sanctuary lamp. He passed in front of the home of one of his old friends while a banquet was in progress, like those he had once hosted and at which he had been applauded by all. The contrast between what he had been and what he was now doing was so striking that he almost lost heart again, and all but asked himself: "What's the use of all this?"

But again he overcame the terrible temptation and begged a little oil from his friends, confessing to them the moment of weakness he had just experienced.

The work of restoring St. Damian's was followed by a similar effort on the ancient Benedictine church of St. Peter, and then on the small, rustic chapel of Portiuncula. And each time Francis changed his place of residence, if so we can call it. He had no fixed dwelling, and usually found some shelter for the night close to the place he was engaged in rebuilding. He truly believed this was his life's mission.

He sang and prayed as he worked. He prayed night and day. The days passed very quickly. Whenever he could, he would attend the holy Sacrifice of the Mass. Much later, he was to write in his *Testament* these words that reveal his favorite devotion:

"Here on earth I see only the most holy body and blood of the Son of God. I shall therefore honor these sacred mysteries above everything else."

And it was during a eucharistic celebration that he heard words that would change his life once more. The hour was near, though he didn't know it, when God was preparing wings for him and would give him brothers to share in his work. New horizons would be opened up for them that would have a great and beneficial influence on the future of the Church. From a builder of churches, he was to become a mainstay of the universal Church.

THE FIRST DISCIPLES — A NEW MISSION

The Gospel of St. Matthias

We have now come to February 24, 1209. It was almost two years since Francis had solemnly broken off with his father and the world. He was known in the city as the builder of churches, but probably had more detractors than admirers. He knew that many considered him crazy, and he accepted to be called "the madman of the Lord." Courageously, in the most absolute solitude of soul, he continued on his way, entrusting the mystery of his future to God alone.

That day was the feast of St. Matthias, apostle. Francis went to Mass in his little chapel of Portiuncula, which had been restored through his efforts.

According to Wadding, the learned historiographer of the Franciscan Order, it was the old priest of St. Damian's, Francis' friend, who had agreed to go and say Mass at the Portiuncula. In those days, the Gospel that was read on the feast of St. Matthias was the following:

"As you go, make this announcement: 'The reign of God is at hand!' Cure the sick, raise the dead, heal the leprous, expel demons. The gift you have received, give as a gift. Provide yourselves with neither gold nor silver nor copper in your belts; no traveling bag, no change of shirt, no sandals, no walking staff. The workman, after all, is worth his keep.

"Look for a worthy person in every town or village you come to and stay with him until you leave. As you enter his home bless it. If the home is deserving, your blessing will descend on it. If it is not, your blessing will return to you" (Mt. 10:7-13).

That particular day, Francis was so wonderfully attuned to these words that he felt their impact as never before. He was to write in his *Testament* shortly before his death, as he remembered this page of the Gospel: "The Most High Himself deigned to reveal to me that I was to live by the holy Gospel.... God Himself revealed to me the formula of salutation we must give and which is the following: 'May the Lord give you peace!'"

According to Celano, after Mass he had a decisive talk with the old priest and said to him, referring to the Gospel of the day: "This is what I want to do with all my might."

Francis was not renouncing his role as "rebuilder," but taking on the role of *evangelist* as well. He felt he was called to repeat to everyone: "Reform your lives! The reign of God is at hand" (Mt. 3:2). Celano interprets it this way: "He preached the kingdom of God and penance, while constantly exulting in the inebriation of the divine Spirit." *The Three Companions* says the same thing, affirming that he "eagerly accepted this mission of apostleship and penance."

Beyond any doubt Francis had just passed another "turning point." The road was becoming clearer to him. He entered with enthusiasm into the ways of his Lord.

The first disciple

So "the Lord's madman" began to preach in Assisi. He went about it very simply in the public squares, in the streets, in the marketplace, everywhere he saw people. And his first words touched the passers-by: *"May the Lord give you His peace!"* People would look at him and come closer. They weren't laughing anymore. They listened, nodded in approval, and began to agree with him. The things he said were so true. And what was he saying? That we must remain at peace with God, with our neighbor, and with ourselves. And this young man had so much inner conviction, such flaming love, that the fire spread to others. Jesus had said this before him: "I have come to light a fire on the earth" (Lk. 12:49).

According to Celano, his first recruit was "a simple and devout man of Assisi," but nothing more is known of him, not even his name. The first recorded disciple was a young merchant from a wealthy family by the name of Bernard di Quintavalle. The *Fioretti*, or *The Little Flowers of St. Francis*, a delightful collection of legends based on truth, point to him as "Francis' first companion," and call him Bernard of Assisi. The story is told that Bernard wanted to get some idea of Francis' real piety, so he invited him to supper and to spend the night.

Bernard laid a trap for Francis. He prepared a bed for him in his own room, which was lighted with an oil lamp. Francis, unaware of his friend's plans,

Byzantine-style crucifix before which St. Francis
was praying when he heard the words: "Go and
rebuild my house...."

Statue of St. Francis in the tiny cell where—
according to tradition—the young man was im-
prisoned by his father after having sold some of
his merchandise in order to rebuild St. Damian's.

The Chiesa Nuova (New Church), built over
St. Francis' paternal home.

Wood-carvings and miniature in the sacristy of
the Basilica of St. Mary of the Angels. These
date back to the early days of the Franciscan Order.

Chapel of the Tears at St. Mary of the Angels.
This painting commemorates St. Francis' devotion
to the Passion of Christ. According to legend,
roses sprang up where the saint's tears fell.

View of Assisi today. Parts of the city have changed little since the time of St. Francis.

Thornless rosebushes at St. Mary of the Angels. According to tradition, the saint cast himself into rosebushes in order to rid himself of a strong temptation, and when he did so the thorns disappeared.

Facade of the Portiuncula, a chapel dating back to the sixth century. This was a favorite place of prayer for St. Francis and his followers.

Painting of St. Francis' passage to heaven, on the outer wall of the chapel marking the site where he died.

The Portiuncula Chapel, since the sixteenth
century enclosed within the Basilica
of St. Mary of the Angels.

St. Francis' tomb in the crypt of the thirteenth-
century basilica that bears his name. Niches in
the walls of the crypt contain the tombs of
Brothers Leo, Masseo, Rufino and Angelo.

Another artist's conception of the death
of St. Francis.

The "Madonna of the Sunset" in the Basilica of St. Francis. At sunset the painting is illuminated by rays filtering through a facing window. Many interpretations have been given to this pleasant scene of the Madonna and Child, St. Francis and St. John.

Well at the cloister of St. Damian's (the convent of St. Clare and her first sisters).

Habit of St. Francis, preserved in the basilica
that bears his name.

Statue of St. Francis in the rose garden at
St. Mary of the Angels. Birds frequently perch
or nest in the statue's hands.

threw himself on the bed and made believe he was sound asleep. Bernard did the same, even snoring loudly.

Fooled by the snoring, Francis quietly got up and began to pray. His hands and eyes were raised to heaven. In a whisper, he kept repeating a single invocation with great fervor: "My God! My God!" And tears ran down his cheeks. That went on until morning. Bernard, who was watching Francis' every move, kept on snoring so as not to interrupt him. And the whispered prayer continued: "My God! My God!" According to the *Fioretti*, Francis was deep in contemplation; he was praising the excellence of the divine Majesty who had condescended to come into the world at the risk of death to bring salvation to the soul of His *poverello*, Francis, and to the souls of many others through him.

Meanwhile Bernard was pondering the idea of joining forces with this man. The next morning, he said to him: "Brother Francis, my heart is completely disposed to abandon the world and follow you in anything you may command."

But Francis said that this would require serious thought, much prayer, and then they would have to go to the bishopric where a holy priest would say Mass for them. Afterward, they would consult God's will by opening the missal three times, to discover what God wanted. And so it was done. The priest said Mass and blessed them. Then Francis opened the missal at random, making "the very holy Sign of the Cross." The first time the missal was opened, they came upon the words: "If you seek perfection, go, sell your possessions, and give to the poor.... Afterward, come back and follow me" (Mt. 19:21).

The second time the missal was opened, they came upon these words spoken to the apostles: "Provide yourselves with neither gold nor silver nor copper in your belts; no traveling bag, no change of

shirt, no sandals, no walking staff" (Mt. 10:9-10). And
the third time, the words were: "If a man wishes to
come after me, he must deny his very self, take up
his cross, and begin to follow in my footsteps"
(Mt. 16:24).

Without a moment's delay, Bernard went to the
public square in front of the church of St. George,
and began distributing everything he owned to
widows, orphans, prisoners, the sick, and pilgrims.
Francis stood nearby, quivering with joy that he had
found such a generous companion. About that time,
a priest named Silvester came by. He had sold stones
to Francis to rebuild St. Damian's. When he saw this
show of generosity, he complained he had been paid
so little for the stones. Francis didn't hesitate a
minute. Taking a handful of gold from Bernard's
pocket, he held it out to the priest, saying: "Now,
are you paid in full, sir priest?" Silvester took the
sum without a word, but he was so deeply troubled
that he soon came back to place himself under
Francis' guidance. He became "Brother Silvester."

Before Silvester, who was the first priest in
the group, others had already come to join Francis.
We know their names. First, there was Peter Catani,
one of Bernard's friends; then the delightful *Egidio* —
or Giles, in English. And there were the first "penitents," as they called themselves: Sabbatino, Morico,
and a certain John *di Capella,* so-called because he
wore a hat.

When they were in Assisi, they sought shelter
in a hut made of branches, near the Portiuncula
chapel. But most of the time they were on the road,
preaching in the area of the Marches of Ancona, or
in the Rieti valley in the Sabine Mountains. Francis
was so well pleased with the friends God had given
him that he called them "his knights of the Round
Table," showing that he still had the spirit of chivalry. For their part, his companions had great love and

respect for him. When he would finish preaching, gentle Brother Giles could not help adding: "What he is telling you is the truth. Listen carefully and do what he tells you."

Mission followed upon mission. Soon four new companions joined the six who were already part of Francis' troupe. These were Philip Lonzo, John di San Costanzo, Barbaro and Bernard di Vigilanzio. The eleventh companion was a young knight from Riety, Angelo Tancredi, whom Francis had accosted one day and addressed abruptly: "You have worn the belt, the sword, and spurs long enough! It is time now to change the belt for the cord, the sword for the cross of Christ, spurs for the dust and mud of the highroads. Follow me, and I'll make you a knight in Christ's army."

His words proved irresistible.

Means of subsistence

Including Francis, there were twelve brothers. When they were not out on missions, they gathered near Assisi, their rallying point. Two problems now arose: the problems of food and lodging. The latter was quickly solved. As their crude shack at Portiuncula was too small, they settled close by at Rivo-Torto in a few dilapidated hovels.

But the question of subsistence was more delicate. People were growing tired of offering them charity. Although most of the brothers had been rich, they had sold everything and given to the poor. They were accused of wanting to live at the expense of the public. Bishop Guido had kept in close touch with the movement from its origins, and thought it was his duty to intervene. Calling Francis, he tried to make him understand that he must assure his companions means of subsistence.

At first Francis was surprised, but quickly regained his composure and answered with a smile: "My Lord, if we possess property, then we shall need arms to defend it, for it will be the cause of quarrels and lawsuits, and in the end it will turn us away from love of God and neighbor."

What could the bishop answer? At that very moment, he was having difficulties of his own with various religious communities concerning certain episcopal properties.

And yet Francis could not fail to see that a degree of organization was necessary. The only point on which he was adamant was the matter of *poverty*. In his *Testament* he was to explain how the problem was settled:

"We were very simple in spirit and subject to everyone. I worked with my hands, as I intend to continue to do. And I want all the other brothers also to practice an honorable trade. Those who don't know any will have to learn one, whatever it may be, not out of desire for gain but to give good example and not remain idle. And it is only when we receive no remuneration for our work that we must turn to the table of our Lord, that is to say, go door to door asking alms."

This passage is very clear. There were to be two means of subsistence: first of all work, for the sole purpose of maintaining life, and, when that was lacking, the "table of our Lord," that is to say, public charity.

Francis had not forgotten St. Paul's words: "Anyone who would not work should not eat" (2 Thes. 3:10). Indeed, he cited this text in his *Testament*. He therefore made it a rule that the brothers, during the intervals between their missions, should help the peasants in the fields when there was need. From that time on, the brothers were seen harvesting the crops in season. Brother Giles gathered grapes in the vineyards, and also crops of nuts. Others gathered fagots which were exchanged for provisions. Francis gave the example. We know he had no aversion to work, in fact, quite the contrary. This he had certainly shown in his efforts to rebuild the churches. But his outstanding ability lay in fashioning all sorts of wooden utensils.

The essential for all the brothers was to remain in the spirit of poverty. They received the bread they needed for their subsistence, but they never forgot the poor, especially those in the leper hospital, who had always remained dear to Francis' heart.

In cases of extreme need, they had recourse to the alms they could obtain from passers-by or in house-to-house begging. This was the most humiliating way of providing for their needs, but they continued to bless what Francis loved to call "the table of our Lord."

The journey to Rome in 1210

A new inspiration came to Francis, perhaps at the suggestion of his excellent bishop. He would ask Rome to approve a "way of life" for himself and his followers.

Obviously, this "way of life" had to be set down in rough outline in one way or another. It was what we would now call a *Rule*. We learn from his own *Testament* that he wrote or dictated such a document: "I myself had someone write down in a few simple words what the Lord Pope had confirmed for me." Celano tells us the same thing in his turn, for we read in his *Chronicles* of the Order: "He wrote a Rule, in which he inserted almost all the commandments Christ had once given to the apostles."

This Rule has been lost, and we must not confuse it with what has been called "the first Rule," written in 1221, that is, eleven years later. In fact, it contained only passages from the Gospels. But Francis, as a dedicated man of the Church, wanted even these to be approved personally by the Pope.

It was probably during the summer of 1210 that Francis and his eleven companions set out from Rivo-Torto for Rome. There they encountered their own Bishop Guido. It had no doubt been decided upon in advance. In any case, Guido recommended them to the care of Cardinal John of St. Paul, a member of the noble Colonna family.

From the canonical point of view, nothing could have been more important than this episcopal recommendation. Rome could not ignore it. What was at stake here? The Cardinal, at the request of the bishop of Assisi, immediately sought to find out. He found a group of shabbily dressed young men, for the most part laymen. Their leader, Francis, was then twenty-eight years old. It was abundantly clear that he was full of love for Jesus Christ, totally submissive to the Church. When he was asked what he wanted, he answered, according to an ancient text: "God has called us to come to the help of His holy Faith, as well as to the help of the clerics and priests of the Roman Church."

A few days later, the Cardinal agreed to transmit Francis' request to the Pope. At that time the Pope was Innocent III, considered one of the great Pontiffs of Christian history. He was eminently qualified to understand Francis and God's plans for him. And so the Cardinal said to him: "I have found a man of very high perfection who has resolved to live according to the precepts of the Church and to observe the Gospel ideal to the letter. It is my view that the Lord really wants to use this man to renew the holy Catholic Faith throughout the Church." How could a Pope refuse to receive such a man personally and without delay?

Visit to the Pope

According to the collected testimonies concerning this audience, we get the following picture. At the Pope's invitation, Francis set forth his program and his hopes.

"My very dear son," the Pope answered, "I find the life you and your brothers are leading too hard. I do not doubt that in the first burst of enthusiasm you can certainly continue to live this way for a time. But you must think of those who will come after you. They may not have the same zeal and will not be sustained by the same fervor."

"My Lord Pope," Francis answered, "I entrust everything to my Lord Jesus Christ. He has promised us eternal life in eternal beatitude. How could He refuse to give us the little we need to live on this earth?"

"What you say, my dear son, is indeed true, but don't forget that human nature is weak and rarely remains in the same state. Go, my son, and ask God to reveal to you in what measure your desires are in harmony with His holy will."

They are both right, really. Francis felt he was sustained by divine grace. Innocent III seemed to have foreseen what would inevitably happen, and what was to dominate the whole history of Franciscanism. Was not the ideal Francis had conceived and willed in great part superhuman?

When the Pope discussed the matter with his council in a consistory, doubts and objections came to light. Wasn't Francis proposing something contradictory? On the one hand he asked the permission to preach, and on the other permission to practice absolute poverty. But in order to preach, one must prepare oneself by study, and in order to study, there must be houses, libraries, books. Certainly each of the members of the new group was free to embrace poverty, as in the Rules of the ancient Orders. But it was impossible that the group as a whole should renounce the means of providing for its students and preachers.

To all these objections, John Cardinal Colonna of St. Paul kept answering: "This man is asking permission to live according to the rules of the Gospel. If we declare this plan to be beyond human strength, we are likewise proclaiming that it is impossible for any man to follow the Gospel. This will make us liable to the accusation that we are outraging Christ, who is the first and true inspirer of the Sacred Book."

That was the language of Christian logic. Had apostolic life really existed or not? And if it had once existed, why should it have become impracticable now?

So Francis was summoned once more to the Lateran palace where the Pope resided.

The Pope's dream

It was during the night preceding this second audience that the Pope had the dream told by Francis' biographers. There was nothing unusual about it. There had been a lively discussion at the consistory. Innocent III could not help being deeply concerned about the great question he had submitted to the cardinals' judgment. There should be no surprise that he dreamed about it. It is entirely possible that in his dream he formulated the answer he wanted to give Francis.

The dream was this: The Pope saw the great Lateran basilica, the "head and mother of all the churches," tottering on its foundations. In his terror, he wanted to cry out, or at the very least join his hands in prayer, but he could not. And then he saw a poor man coming toward him on the Lateran

Square, clothed in peasant's attire, a tunic tied with a belt, and his feet bare. Without looking to the left or the right, this poor man walked straight toward the crumbling basilica. He leaned against the falling walls, and suddenly there was a miracle. He held them up and put the structure back on its foundations. In his dream, the sleeping Pope began to breathe more easily. But he was amazed to discover, when the poor peasant turned slightly to the side, that he was none other than the little brother from Assisi, the same Francis who was asking permission to renew the way of life of Christ's first apostles: permission to work and preach in absolute poverty!

How has the Pope's dream come down to us? There is no mention of it in the oldest biographies of our saint. But according to the Franciscan historiographer Wadding, Innocent III told the dream to his own nephew, Cardinal Richard Hannibal di Molaria, who died in 1274. The Cardinal in turn is said to have transmitted it to Brother Jerome di Ascoli, who succeeded St. Bonaventure as Minister General of the Order in 1274. Jerome di Ascoli, who served as Pope from 1288 to 1292 under the name of Nicholas IV, commanded that this episode be inserted into the text of the biography of St. Francis written by St. Bonaventure.

There was, we see, a quasi-official interpolation into the text which was included only in those manuscripts which could be revised. This explains why it is absent from some of the manuscripts. We can nevertheless express our faith in this account, given its origin as described above.

It is certain that the Pope gave Francis his approbation, after the hesitations and objections we have seen. According to Celano, he said to Francis, surrounded by his brothers: "My brothers, go with God and preach conversion to everyone, as the Lord will inspire you. And when the Almighty has mul-

tiplied your number, come back to me without fear
and you will find me disposed to grant you still more
and to entrust even greater tasks to you."

At these words, they all knelt before the Pope
and swore obedience to him. But he in turn asked
them to swear obedience to Francis as their head.
The Pope granted only to Francis the permission to
preach, but with the right to transmit this permission, under his own responsibility, to those of his
brothers whom he deemed capable of it. It was understood that instead of remaining in the lay state the
brothers would be incorporated into the clergy by
ecclesiastical tonsure, conferred on them then and
there by Cardinal of St. Paul, who was now one of
their most active and powerful protectors.

The return to Rivo-Torto

It was with great joy, therefore, that Francis
and his brothers returned home. During these early
days when they still had no official name, they were
sometimes called the "Grey Penitents" of Assisi.
The Pope had given only a verbal approbation. But
it had been given in the presence of irrefutable witnesses, and first of all, John Cardinal Colonna, who
must have told Bishop Guido of Assisi about it. This
was ample support for the initial departure. Soon
Francis and his brothers were back in their convent
at Rivo-Torto. As we know, this was only a crude
hut, or *tugurium,* according to our sources. The news
that the group had been approved by the Pope could
not be kept secret. It immediately spread over the
countryside, and this led Francis and his brothers to
talk about it more confidently.

So the preaching began anew, and produced
incomparable fruit. New followers joined the group.
The first to join the "Penitents" was the priest
Silvester whose story we told earlier. He was the first
priest of the newborn Order. In this capacity he was

certainly welcomed with special delight, and thus the celebration of the Holy Mysteries was assured within the group from that moment.

Abundant fruit

All our sources, especially Celano's *First Biography* and *The Three Companions*, attest that Francis began a series of preaching tours in the churches of the area, including the cathedral of Assisi, and that his sermons produced a wave of admiration among the people and many conversions. *The Three Companions* tell us that "many persons, with the Spirit of God, threw off all temporal cares and walked in the paths the saint opened up for them."

A brilliant example of this was the entrance into religion of the noble lady Clare Offreduccio, which we shall soon recount.

Recruits were increasing among the brothers. But even those who had no thought of becoming religious felt transformed by God's grace and uplifted by the words of St. Francis and his followers.

One of the outstanding results of this campaign of preaching was probably the solemn and official reconciliation that occurred in Assisi between the *"majores"* and the *"minores"*—which we might translate as "nobles" and "lower classes." On November 9, 1210, a few months after Francis' return from Rome with his brothers, a genuine *Municipal Charter* was signed. It was a perpetual covenant among all the inhabitants of the city. We must remember that, at that period of history, cities were divided into many factions, which were always at each others' throats. It seems very likely, therefore, that the attainment of social peace in Assisi was the work of someone in particular, and that this was very probably the preacher who had become so popular in his native city. Who else, indeed, but Francis, the leader of the *Grey Penitents?*

In any event, the new Charter certainly bore the mark of the Christian religion, for it opened with these words:

"In the name of God. Amen. May the grace of the Holy Spirit be with you! In honor of our Lord Jesus Christ, of the Blessed Virgin Mary, of Emperor Otto and Duke Leopold...."

Besides, we are sure that, while Francis avoided discussing dogmatic questions from the pulpit as he was not well enough educated, he always extolled peace. His watchword, which was to remain that of his Order, was already *Pax et Bonum: Peace and all good things!* The famous legend about the wolf of Gubbio, related in the *Fioretti,* has long been thought to be about the conversion of a noble from Gubbio who had behaved like a "wolf" throughout the area and, thanks to Francis, became gentle as a lamb. This, in turn, led to a "peace" analogous to that which was concluded in Assisi.

The Friars Minor

It was probably during the same year, 1210, that Francis finally gave his community a distinctive name, that was to come down to us through the centuries. Celano tells us about it in this way:

One day Francis and his brothers were listening to a rereading of their "way of life," written by him and approved by the Pope. We know it consisted almost entirely of words from the Gospels. But it seems to have included the following sentence addressed to those who wanted to apply this rule: "And let them be the lowliest among men—*et sint minores!*" Now Francis had long been seeking an appropriate name for himself and his brothers. This time he was struck by the words as he heard them reread. Until then, the group had been called "the Penitents of Assisi" or "the Grey Penitents" because of the color of their tunics. But this was only a temporary name.

Inspired by the term *minores*, Francis suddenly cried out: "Minors, that is to say, very lowly brothers, brothers inferior to all other men! Surely, that name suits me and my followers! We shall be the *Friars Minor*." And this name was adopted for them all. It remained the name of the Order during its formative period, and when definitive approbation was received from Rome, it was also accepted by general usage. Just as Dominic de Guzman founded the Order of the *Friars Preachers* about this time, so Francis founded the Order of the *Friars Minor*. History was to set the two side by side, as the first of the four mendicant Orders. The other two were to be the Carmelites and the Augustinians.

At Portiuncula

The brothers' stay at Rivo-Torto ended in the most unexpected way. One day when the "minors" were in their wretched shed, each praying and meditating in his own place, a peasant suddenly and unceremoniously barged into the *tugurium* followed by his donkey, to whom he shouted: "Come on in, my donkey, we can settle down comfortably here!"

Anyone else but Francis might have been angered by this rude intrusion. But with the patience and gentleness he had received from his Jesus, Francis merely looked at the peasant for a moment, and when he realized he intended to transform this refuge of prayer into a stable, he got up and said as serenely as possible to his followers: "It is certainly true, my brothers, that God has not called us to maintain an inn for donkeys, but to pray and show other men the path to salvation."

They all understood what he meant, and immediately left Rivo-Torto, never to return. It mattered not to them that this hut had become very dear to them because of the graces they had received there. They set out toward Portiuncula, whose church had always been their favorite center for prayer, and this was to be the site of their "motherhouse," if we dare call it so.

The very modest chapel of Portiuncula is still venerated today, although it is now enclosed within a vast basilica. In those days, it belonged to the Camaldolese monks of Mount Subiaso, as did the grounds surrounding it. Francis and his brothers were delighted when the Camaldolese gave them permission to settle down in this place that Francis held so dear and whose chapel he had rebuilt.

It was early in 1211 when the "Friars Minor" came to live near the chapel. They needed neither architect, nor trained builders to help them. They simply set to work building a cabin of interlaced branches, plastered with mud and covered over with leaves. For their night's rest, they laid straw-filled sacks out on the floor. Their enclosure consisted of a rudimentary hedge. The furnishings—tables and chairs—were reduced to a minimum. We can imagine nothing poorer and more denuded. Here the Franciscan ideal was expressed in all its austerity.

Among the brothers who had come to swell the size of the community, there were several who would also be included in the magnificent legend of the Order: Brothers Rufino, Masseo, and Juniper, and, above all, Brother Leo, who was to be one of Francis' most diligent companions and would be known as "little lamb of God."

But the most remarkable "lamb" who came to join the Friars Minor at this time was Clare Offreduccio, whose exciting story we shall now relate.

CLARE OFFREDUCCIO AND THE FRANCISCAN SECOND ORDER

Clare's youth

The woman we honor by the
beloved name of St. Clare belonged
to a noble family of Assisi.
Careful studies have been made
of her life in recent years, and
historians have reached definitive
conclusions about her through
their research.

Until quite recently, her father
was called Favorino Scifi. It has
been proven that his name was
really Faverone di Offreduccio.
Her mother, Ortolana, likewise of
noble birth, came from Serpeto,
a village close to Assisi.

The couple had five children:
Boso, Penenda, Clare, Agnes,
and Beatrice. We are told that
Ortolana had made many pil-
grimages, disregarding the dangers
involved. She is said to have
gone as far as Jerusalem, and that
was considered a real adventure.
She brought her children up in
the practice of the most fervent

piety, training them in a spirit of humility, penance, and especially charity toward the poor.

Clare, or *Chiara* as she was called in Italian, spent her earliest years by the side of her mother and sisters. No one could have guessed what would become of this young girl who grew in beauty and charm with each passing year. Her recollected attitude at church, and her eagerness to visit the poorest homes of the city were general knowledge.

Until recently, the date of her birth was supposed to have been January 20, 1194, but historians have now set the year as 1193.

We should note that Clare's family, related to most of the noble families of Assisi, was among those that had to seek refuge in Perugia from 1200 to 1205, after engaging in a conflict with the burghers and the lower classes. When Faverone and his family returned to Assisi, Clare was twelve years old, and from that time on the family was anxious to marry her off. Very desirable suitors came forward. In fact, the only problem was one of choice. But Clare energetically turned down every offer of marriage.

Again in 1210, five years later, her parents spoke to her of a suitor much to their liking. It was then that Clare declared she had no intention of getting married. Her parents were dumbfounded. When pressed, she finally admitted to her mother that she had secretly consecrated herself to God and therefore could not contract any marriage. Even for such good Christians as Faverone and Ortolana, such a decision appeared to be a catastrophe. No one had ever penetrated the secrets of this fiery young soul, not even her mother. Her parents reacted forcefully, even violently, against their daughter's plans. They could not budge her.

Francis' influence on Clare

Let us recall the influence Francis had come to wield at about this time. The whole city of Assisi was talking about him, about his rupture with his family and with the world; the strange things he had done at first, which most people considered to be obvious signs of insanity; his amazing perseverance; the wisdom of his observations; his fiery zeal; the intensity of his love for Jesus Christ and the poor, including lepers.

Little by little, day after day, all these things had revolutionized the entire city. Francis was not alone any more. He had found disciples, admirers, companions. Everyone knew that the Pope had received them and approved of what they were doing. The bishop of Assisi had opened his churches to Francis, the preacher. And Francis talked only of love, pure love, love for Christ crucified, love for the lowly and the humble, love among all members of the Christian community.

It was precisely in the year 1210, when Clare Offreduccio's family was concerned with marrying her off, that Francis preached in the church of St. George in Assisi, now known as the church of St. Clare. Among those whose souls would be touched most deeply by Francis' words was Clare. It was as if Jesus Himself were speaking to her from the pulpit, through the lips of Francis. Clare wanted to go and see him, to consult with him privately. This was not an easy thing to do. Her parents were totally opposed to her vocation. But Clare's resolve was unshakable, for it had been formed in the grace of the Holy Spirit. With the help of a relative, Bona del Guelfuccio, Clare found a way of meeting Francis, who was himself accompanied by Brother Philip the Tall. Clare told Francis his ideal of poverty had completely won her over. She, too, wanted to live according to the Gospel, in the pure love of poverty like her Jesus!

Could Francis turn aside a request that conformed so closely to God's will, as he understood it? He didn't think so. It was decided he would talk to the bishop about it, to obtain the necessary powers to receive the Offreduccios' daughter into religious life.

When everything was settled, Francis made a rendezvous with her in the Portiuncula chapel, where the Franciscan community now held its services. In the traditional chronology, Clare's arrival at Portiuncula occurred on Palm Sunday of the year 1212. But more recent historians (Fathers Lazzei and Bracaloni) believe the event occurred on March 27, 1211, which was also a Palm Sunday. The earlier date has likewise been adopted by Bastianini.

Clare receives the habit

Clare wanted to bid the world farewell in the most solemn way, even if in secret. On Palm Sunday, therefore, she put on her most expensive gown and went to the cathedral church of Assisi with her mother and sisters. No one in the throng of women and young girls shone with as much beauty and elegance as the blonde Clare Offreduccio.

The story is told that when the blessed palms were distributed, when everyone else was going up to the front to receive a small olive branch from the bishop, only Clare remained in her place. No doubt she was lost in thought and as if in ecstasy anticipating what she planned to do that very night. But the bishop, no doubt informed of what was to happen, understood the drama unfolding in this privileged young soul. So he brought Clare her palm in the rear of the church.

At dusk of that same day, Clare made her escape. She was fleeing her father's house in obedience to a divine call. With her own hands she removed a large pile of wood obstructing a hidden door, and slipped out with her friend Bona Guelfuccio. Soon they were on the road to Portiuncula, which is about a half-hour's walk from the city, out in the plain. The Franciscan friars had been waiting, and came out to meet her with torches. Soon, kneeling before the venerated image of the Virgin Mary in the little chapel, Clare pronounced the promises that detached her from the world. She herself said she did this "out of love for the very holy and dear Child, wrapped in poor swaddling clothes and lying in the manger."

A great mystery of sacred love had just unfolded. Henceforth Clare would call herself "the unworthy servant of Christ and the little plant of Blessed Father Francis." Clare gave the friars her glittering dress, receiving in its place a wool smock, similar to those the friars wore. She exchanged her belt, adorned with jewels, for a simple knotted cord. Her beautiful hair fell under Francis' scissors, and she covered her head with a black veil. Her feet were shod in simple wooden sandals. Then she pronounced the three vows of religion. And so the Order of the *Poor Ladies* was born, that would later be called the Order of the *Poor Clares* and the *Franciscan Second Order*.

At St. Damian's

However, a problem arose: where would Francis' "first plant" be lodged? There was no convent yet to receive her. Nor could she be placed all by herself into any available dwelling. But Francis, no doubt after consultation with the bishop, had made provisions for this. That very night after the ceremony at Portiuncula, Clare was taken to the Benedictine nuns of St. Paul of Abbatissis, at Bastia, not far from Assisi. She was to remain there "as long as Providence had no other plans for her."

Inevitably there was great excitement in Assisi over the news that Clare Offreduccio had left her family's house. Faverone's brother Monaldo, who considered himself the head of the family, was particularly incensed. It was generally believed the young girl had entered a convent, since she had expressed the firm intention of doing so. But where? Efforts were made to find out, and soon it was learned she was at the monastery of St. Paul. So Monaldo arrived there, his lips full of threats, and determined, as he said, to "dissuade his niece from this vile action!"

He was most indignant when he saw that he was powerless against Clare's stubbornness. In a frenzy of anger, he decided to use force. But Clare suddenly uncovered her forehead and revealed her shaved head to remind him that now she belonged to God and he could not touch her without coming under the ban of excommunication.

Thus disarmed, Monaldo returned to Assisi without bringing Clare back to her parents. But after this dramatic incident Francis thought it better to take the young nun to the Benedictine convent of Panzo in Assisi. There, he must have thought, it was easier to claim the bishop's sovereign protection in case of need, for all that had happened thus far had been with the prelate's permission.

Just sixteen days after Clare's clothing at the Portiuncula, her sister Agnes came to join her at the convent of Panzo to be consecrated to Lady Poverty. This time Monaldo's anger knew no bounds. He arrived at the convent with armed men to snatch Agnes away before she had a chance to pronounce any vows. The terrified Benedictine nuns bowed to the force of arms and delivered the young girl to her uncle. Meanwhile, Clare was powerless to help, so she retired into her cell to pray. Agnes, still a child, resisted with all her strength and kept on screaming: "Clare, Clare, come and help me!" But Clare could only besiege her Jesus with prayers.

And suddenly the miracle happened. The twelve hefty men who were dragging poor Agnes away were stricken with an inexplicable weakness. They couldn't move the girl's frail body an inch. The exasperated Monaldo then raised his iron-gloved fist over the child's head as if to crush it with a single blow. But his arm remained as though petrified and paralyzed. It was now his turn to beg for mercy. So young Agnes was released, half-dead with fright. God had spoken, indeed He had spoken so loudly that soon Clare's third sister Beatrice hastened to join her older sisters. Better still, their mother Ortolana would become a nun after her husband's death, in the same Order as her daughters, accepting to obey Clare as her superior.

Meanwhile Francis had obtained from Bishop Guido of Assisi permission to install his nuns close to the chapel of St. Damian, where he had first heard God's voice.

After spending four months with the Benedictine nuns of Panzo (officially known as the nuns of San Angelo di Pace), the *Poor Ladies* settled at St. Damian's.

We shall briefly relate the beginnings of their community, which now complemented that of the *Friars Minor* at Portiuncula.

The rule of poverty

We have already pointed out that Clare di Offreduccio had indeed been conquered by Francis' own ideal, which was to live the Gospel to the

letter. Clare seemed even more aflame with this
desire, if that were possible, than her holy director. At her request, therefore, Francis wrote what
he called a "way of life," that is to say, a Rule, in the
same spirit as the one the Pope had approved in
1210. This was the first Rule of St. Damian. Although
this text has been lost, its substance has been preserved in Chapter VI of the Rule Clare later wrote.
Absolute poverty was demanded. Every person
wishing to enter the Order must first distribute all
her possessions to the poor. Clare was the first to
divest herself of her paternal inheritance by giving
it to the poor. She also had her sister Agnes' possessions sold. It was decided they would live only
by the work of their hands and by whatever alms
they could collect.

Clare clung so resolutely to her ideal that
she was not satisfied until she obtained from Pope
Innocent III what she called *"the privilege of poverty."* By this she meant the canonical right to possess neither property nor income in the convent or
anywhere in the Order. While this concession by
the Pope has sometimes been denied, recent studies
prove that he did in fact make it.

According to Cristofari, the document enact-
ing this "privilege" was signed by Innocent III
while on a visit to Perugia, some time between
June 1 and July 16, 1216. Another historian thinks
the year was more probably 1215. That same year,
at Francis' wish and in conformity with the regulations of the Lateran Council of 1215, Clare was
given a new title and consecrated as abbess. But
even the most sacred titles were for her only an
added reason for humbling herself more than all
the other nuns by sharing in their labors and pen-
ances, as well as giving them the example of poverty and sacrifice, most difficult for human nature.

The expansion of the Order

In the troubled society of the early thirteenth century, there was a burning thirst to imitate Jesus Christ. Just as young men came from everywhere to be under Francis' direction, so too young ladies came to place themselves under Clare's authority and guidance. We know the names of many of these earliest Poor Clares. First of all, there were the friends and relatives of the newly-consecrated twenty-two-year-old abbess. We have already spoken of her third sister, and even of her mother. But many other relatives came to join the original nucleus.

A serious difficulty arose when Cardinal Hugolino, the future Pope Gregory IX, arrived in the area as the legate of Pope Honorius III, to make his canonical visitation of the monasteries. He tried to make the Poor Clares accept a Rule to his liking, that he considered better adapted to human capacities, and especially to the capacities of women. The Lateran Council of 1215 had ordered that new Orders should conform to an already approved Rule, in order to put a stop to what seemed the excessive proliferation of religious Orders. Thus, Cardinal Hugolino's Rule was an adaptation of the Rule of St. Benedict, with certain austerities borrowed from the Cistercian nuns. But there was nothing in his Rule about poverty, that is, about the complete absence of collective ownership of property. At the time, Francis and Clare were obliged to passively accept the new arrangements. But Clare and her nuns remained faithful in practice to the "way of life" written by their father, Francis. And in the secret of her heart Clare resolved not to rest until she had obtained confirmation of her famous privilege of poverty from the Holy See.

It is very moving to think of Clare's obstinate resolve to be as faithful as possible to the Gospel.

One of Francis' sermons

We must not imagine Francis came very often to visit his "daughters." On the contrary, he rarely went to preach God's word to them. And yet Clare loved to hear sermons, for she could not forget that it was through Francis' sermons her own vocation had come into being. One day, when she learned Pope Gregory IX was thinking of prohibiting the Friars Minor from preaching in the monasteries of the Poor Clares, she sent him word that she was going to dismiss the brothers charged with begging bread for the cloistered nuns. She announced to the Pontiff: "If we can abstain from spiritual bread, then we can also abstain from bread for the body!" The Pope understood and withdrew his order.

Under the circumstances we can understand that Clare and her nuns considered it a great blessing when Francis came to St. Damian's to preach to them. Our sources contain a sermon that has remained famous. It was probably given around 1221. Francis entered the convent church and remained for a few moments deep in prayer, his eyes raised heavenward. Then, turning toward the sister sacristan, he asked for some ashes. When he held the ashes in the palm of his hand, he drew a circle around his person in the presence of the nuns who were looking at him from behind their cloister grille. He took what remained of the ashes and poured them on his head. He had not said a single word during this little pantomime.

All the nuns were eagerly awaiting the promised sermon. But Francis simply recited the *Miserere*, Psalm 50, which is the principal penitential psalm. And when he had finished, he left the church still without a word. He was delighted that once again he had reminded his nuns of the great law of penance and that he had made them practice it by missing the sermon they wanted so much to hear.

The privilege of poverty

We know that Cardinal Hugolino had always wanted Clare to renounce the "privilege of poverty," not because he was opposed to it in principle but because he thought such a "privilege" was dangerous for the future of the Order. And he wanted to encourage its growth in every way. When he became Pope in 1227 — a year after the death of Francis of Assisi — he insisted more than ever. In 1228, having come to Assisi to canonize Francis, he again urged his request upon the Mother Abbess of St. Damian's.

But Clare would only answer:

"Holy Father, release me from my sins, but not from the obligation to follow our Lord Jesus Christ!"

Finally, Clare's manifest holiness won out. On September 17, 1228, Gregory IX renewed the privilege he had so long wanted to take from her. The document to this effect is preserved in the church of Santa Chiara in Assisi.

It seems, however, that this privilege was granted to Clare personally. For Gregory IX and his successor made it an obligation for the Poor Clares, under pain of excommunication, to accept the legacies and gifts made to them, and forbade them to give any of them away. Clare persisted in her gentle obstinacy. Between the years 1247 and 1252, she wrote a new Rule, conceived on the model of the Franciscan Rule, and in which absolute poverty was compulsory. The Protector of the Order, Cardinal Raynaldi, approved this Rule in 1252, not for the Order of the Poor Clares as a whole, but at least for the monastery of St. Damian.

Clare's sanctity

We cannot leave "the first plant" of our hero Francis without saying a few words about her own brand of spirituality and her virtues.

It has been said of Clare that she was the perfect expression of Franciscan poverty, modeled on the evangelical conception of Francis of Assisi. In this sense Clare was his most consummate and docile disciple. But how did she visualize poverty? Above all, as an imitation of Christ. The heart of her spirituality was therefore an intense love of Jesus, and of Jesus crucified.

Like Francis, she was constantly meditating on the Savior's passion, and often wept over it. Like Francis, too, she would have wanted to weep in the presence of the whole world at the thought of the sufferings love had inflicted on her Savior. She recited an Office of the Holy Cross, composed by the seraphic Father. One Good Friday, she was in ecstasy, and as though dead to all things, for an entire night and day. Her devotion to the Blessed Sacrament was without equal. At St. Damian's she had an oratory built where the Blessed Sacrament was reserved and where she spent long hours of adoration.

Her mental prayer, that is, her union with God, was continual, and accompanied by lofty mystical favors. True, she never wrote like Teresa of Avila, because she did not feel called by God to do this. But she deserves to be included, with Catherine of Siena and a few other saints, among the great contemplatives of Christian history.

We shall come back to Clare at St. Damian's, at the end of this biography of St. Francis.

But we must once more turn our attention to him, after this necessary digression on a subject of rare beauty.

THE LIFE AND GROWTH OF THE ORDER

Chronological summary

Obviously, it is impossible to relate
in detail everything our sources contain about the new Order. It seems
more practical, therefore, to sum up
what we know of the sequence of
events, and pause afterwards to consider the most important among them.
The first fact we note about the
beginnings of the Order is the
regular assembling of what has been
called the *Chapter of Portiuncula.*
This was a gathering of all the
brothers at Portiuncula, with Francis
presiding. Naturally these chapters
weren't held until the Order had
grown to some size and the brothers
dispersed on various missions. This
necessitated their coming together
at Portiuncula, which, as we have
said, had become a sort of "motherhouse." The date set for the chapter
was Pentecost, a choice that recalled
the gathering of the Apostles after
Christ's death and Ascension. As the
Acts of the Apostles tells us, it was

on Pentecost that all of Christ's "brothers," that is, His disciples numbering about one hundred twenty, were assembled in the Cenacle at Jerusalem. And on that day the Holy Spirit descended upon them and sent them out to preach the Gospel to the whole world.

The Chapter of Pentecost at Portiuncula served as a renewal of the brothers' apostolic zeal. There, Francis could express to all of them the exhortations he had received from the heart of his Divine Master. There, he could draw up plans for missions to be undertaken and for the distribution of various tasks.

The first chapter of this kind took place on Pentecost, 1212. We know of other chapters held in 1214, 1217, 1219, and 1221, all on Pentecost. And we shall return to them.

Principal events

If we cast a glance on the principal ideas and events in the early development of the Order, we shall see one that dominates all the others. It was the eager desire of Francis and his brothers to go and preach the Gospel to the infidels. They didn't limit themselves to exhorting Christians to believe and practice their Faith more perfectly. That was certainly part of their intent, and they devoted themselves to it with all their strength wherever they went. But it was the infidels, and specifically the Saracens in Islamic lands, who haunted Francis' thoughts, and through him the thoughts of all his brothers. They dreamed of preaching Christ in the Orient. They dreamed of fighting a true crusade, one that would not find expression in sword thrusts, or conquests by main strength, but would conquer through preaching, charity, prayer, suffering, the cross, and martyrdom. If God so willed, this was Francis' pure and noble ambition.

We shall see him return to this dream over and over.

Another major event was the Lateran Council of 1215, which Francis attended. There he met Dominic, the distinguished founder of the Friars Preachers.

A chronology of the Order must also include the following events of primary importance:

1. In 1221, the writing of what was to be called the "First Rule," which was to replace the much shorter one we have already mentioned.

2. The institution and approbation of the Third Order, whose amazing benefits we shall soon discuss.

3. In 1223, the writing of the definitive Rule, known as the "Second Rule," approved on November 29 of the same year by Pope Honorius III.

4. On December 25, 1223, the celebration of the feast of Christmas by Francis at Greccio, using a Crèche of the Infant God, the first of its kind.

5. In September, 1224, the famous stigmatization of Francis on Mount Alverna, an event that marks one of the highest peaks of Francis' spiritual life.

6. The writing of the magnificent *Canticle of Creatures,* also known as *The Canticle of Brother Sun*, during the Paschal season of 1225, when Francis was at St. Damian's.

All these events were brought to a climax by the saint's blessed death at Assisi on October 3, 1226.

Now that we have had a glimpse of this short but abundant life, let us go into a little more detail about some of its more significant events.

Colorful episodes

First, we must give our readers a sense of the climate, the atmosphere, in which Francis' brief life unfolded.

Francis lived a delightfully simple life in a spirit of gentle friendliness with all he encountered. A few examples will help us to understand.

This climate was that of the *Fioretti*, with its overtones of legend, dreams, and pure poetry. Here, for instance, is how the story of the vocation of a brother known as John the Simple has come down to us.

While the brothers were still very few in number and living at Portiuncula — probably in 1211 or 1212 — Francis used to go into the towns and villages around Assisi to preach conversion to everyone he met.

He often carried a broom with him to clean the churches that were too terribly neglected. In fact, nothing grieved him more than to find the sanctuary of his God filled with garbage or accumulated dust. Sometimes, when he had finished preaching, he would take the priest of the church aside and ask him in a low voice, so the parishioners could not hear, to see to it that the house of God and the altar of the Holy Sacrifice were resplendent with cleanliness.

One day when he was sweeping and cleaning a church not far from Assisi, word soon spread in the village that he was there. One of the peasants left his oxen in the field he was plowing and came to Francis. This peasant, whose name was John, said to Francis: "Brother, give me your broom and let me help you!" And he soon had finished the job of cleaning the church. Then the two men sat side by side. The peasant said to Francis: "Brother, I have long had the desire to serve God, especially since I heard talk about you and your brothers. But I didn't know where to find you. Now that God has brought me to you, tell me what I must do, because I'm ready to obey you in all things!"

When Francis heard these words, he was over-joyed. He blessed the Lord deep within his soul, and answered: "Brother, if you really mean to live like us, you must first renounce all your possessions and give them to the poor, as it says in the Gospel. All of our brothers have done this, each according to his means."

Without an instant's hesitation, the peasant went back to his oxen, unharnessed them from the plow, and brought them to Francis. Then he said to him: "Brother, for many years I have served my father and the members of my household. I have come to think that one of these oxen was my rightful heritage. I will give that ox to the poor, in the best way you suggest."

But when John's parents heard he was going to leave them, they began to weep long and loud. Francis surmised the real cause for their sorrow, and said to them: "Your son here wants to serve God, and you must certainly not think that is a bad thing. Rather, you should be filled with great joy. But so that you may not be without consolation, I am going to give you this ox that belongs to him and that he wanted to give to the poor, as the Gospel teaches us."

The tears stopped at once. It was the loss of the ox that really concerned them. As for Brother John, he was soon clothed in the habit of the brothers. As he realized he was a very ignorant fellow, he would always get behind Francis and imitate all his move-ments, kneeling or raising his eyes to heaven as he saw Francis doing. When Francis noticed this, he gently reprimanded him. But John the Simple answered: "My brother, I have promised God to do everything you do, and therefore I must imitate you in all things."

Isn't this the moment to exclaim: *O blessed simplicity!*

A beautiful story
from the "Fioretti"

The following story, taken from the *Fioretti,*
or *The Little Flowers of St. Francis,* will carry us
completely back to the Franciscan ambience of the
earliest years.

One day Francis was with Brother Leo (whom
he liked to call his "Brother Leo, little lamb of God"),
in a place where neither of them had a breviary to
recite the Office.

So Francis suggested that they recite a litany
he would compose. "First, I'll say: 'O Brother Francis,
you have done so much evil and committed so many
sins in the world that you deserve to go to hell!'
And you, Brother Leo, are to answer: 'Yes, it's indeed
true that you deserve to go to the depths of hell!'"
So Brother Leo, always obedient and gentle as a dove,
answered: "Yes, that's right, Father. Let us begin
in the name of the Lord!"

Then St. Francis began to say: "O Brother
Francis, you have done so many evil deeds and
committed so many sins in the world that you deserve
to go to hell!"

But Brother Leo answered: "Brother Francis,
God is doing so much good through you that you will
deserve to be received in paradise!"

Francis reprimanded him roundly, saying:
"That's not what you must say, Brother Leo. When
I say: 'Brother Francis, you deserve to be damned!'
you must answer: 'Yes, you certainly deserve to be
among the damned.'" So Brother Leo said: "Very
good, Father."

Then Francis began to sigh and weep, saying:
"O Lord God of heaven and earth, I have committed
so many sins that I deserve to be among the damned."

But Brother Leo answered: "O Brother Francis, God will accomplish such great things through you that you will become a blessed among the blessed."

And Francis was surprised to see that Brother Leo was saying just the opposite of what he had been commanded, and reprimanded him once more: "Why don't you answer as I have told you? In the name of holy obedience, I command you for the last time to answer the way I shall teach you. So, when I say: 'Miserable Francis, how can you believe that God has pity on you when you have committed so many sins against the Father of pity and the God of charity that you deserve no compassion at all?' you, Brother Leo, little lamb of God, must be sure to answer: 'Yes, it's indeed true that you deserve no compassion!'"

Once again Brother Leo promised to do what had been asked of him. But when Francis had spoken the words: "Miserable Francis..." and the rest, Brother Leo replied: "Brother Francis, God the Father, whose compassion is infinitely greater than your sins, will have great pity on you, and besides He will give you many favors!"

When Francis heard this, he was greatly disturbed and not a little irritated. Turning to Brother Leo, he said: "How can you be so disobedient and do exactly the opposite of what I command?"

Then Brother Leo answered very humbly and respectfully: "Father, God is my witness that each time I am willing to answer as you command, but God Himself makes me speak as He pleases and not as I please!"

And while Francis was tearfully begging his disciple to speak as he had told him to, Brother Leo, for all his good intentions and promises, could only say: "O Brother Francis, you will receive a great favor from God, and you will be raised up and glorified for all eternity, because he who humbles himself will be exalted, and it is impossible for me to say anything else. For God Himself is speaking through my lips!"

Perfect joy

Here's another story taken from the *Fioretti*, once again about Francis and his Brother Leo. It concerns something very characteristic of the Order at its origin, namely, *perfect joy*. We find Francis and Leo discussing it in this account.

Actually, the original "Penitents of Assisi" had no intention of living in a spirit of gloom.

The penance they practiced and preached to all comers was not a sullen, downcast penance. It was joyous penance, bathed in the love of Jesus crucified. It was the joy of love, the joy of the beautiful countryside created by God, the joy of being in God's service, the joy of singing God's praises with the angels and the birds! Yes, but also the joy of being humbled before God, as we shall see in the story that has been so often retold.

"One winter night Francis was returning from Perugia to Portiuncula. The cold was bitter and made them both suffer. Leo was walking ahead, lost in his thoughts, when Francis called out to him: 'Brother Leo, even if we were the best examples of holiness and edification in the world, listen carefully and remember what I am telling you: that would still not be perfect joy!'

"The two brothers kept on walking, but after a few more steps Francis again called to his companion: 'Brother Leo, even if we had the power to restore sight to the blind and make paralytics walk, restore speech and hearing to the deaf-mute, or even raise the dead after four days, note well what I tell you: that would still not be perfect joy!'

"For the third time, Francis cried out: 'Brother Leo, if we could speak all languages and know all sciences, and even knew the whole of Scripture by heart, if we could reveal the future and the secrets of men's hearts, listen carefully: that still would not be perfect joy!'

"After going on a little farther, Francis called to his companion and said: 'Brother Leo, little lamb of God, even if we spoke the language of the angels, if we knew the course of the stars and the powers of herbs and plants, even if all the treasures of the earth were known to us and all that concerns the nature of birds, fish, and the other animals, as well as all the properties of trees, waters, and rocks, note carefully what I tell you, Brother Leo: perfect joy would not consist in that!'

"Francis kept on going without saying a word. Then he cried out again: 'O Brother Leo, even if we could preach so well that all infidels were converted to the faith of Christ through our words — pay close attention to what I am telling you — we still wouldn't have perfect joy!'

"Francis kept saying such things until Brother Leo asked him in amazement: 'But, Father, for the love of God, please explain where we could find perfect joy!'

"And Francis answered: 'We shall soon arrive at Portiuncula, wet through with the rain and numb with cold, covered with the mud of the road and exhausted with hunger. Well, now! If the Brother Porter should answer our call and ask us angrily who we were and if, after we told him we were two brothers, he answered: "You are lying, you are nothing but highway robbers who attack people unawares and steal the alms destined for the poor!" — if this brother talks to us in such fashion and refuses to open the door for us; if he leaves us outside, starving in the snow, the rain, and the cold, and if, besides it being dark now, we are patient enough to endure the insults, rebuffs and cruel treatment without becoming angry ourselves, without complaining against this brother porter, and even if, then, humbly and charitably we come to the conclusion that this brother porter knows us very well and God is making him speak against us in this way—listen well, Brother Leo: that would be perfect joy!'

"'And now, suppose we continue to knock and the brother porter is furious, comes out of the house, and treats us like two bothersome rascals and drives us away with blows, shouting: "Go away, you shameless scoundrels, there is no food or shelter for you here!" Well! Brother Leo, if we could still suffer that patiently, cheerfully, and with love, listen well: that would certainly be perfect joy!'

"Then, giving a final commentary on the rather strange things he had said, Francis concluded: 'And now, Brother Leo, I am going to tell you what that means. Beyond all the graces and gifts of the Holy Spirit that God grants to His friends, there is greater joy *in overcoming ourselves and in gladly enduring for the love of Christ every suffering, insult, and injustice.* For we have no right to glory in any of God's other gifts, since they come from Him and not from us, in the words of the Apostle: "Name something you have that you have not received. If, then, you have received it, why are you boasting as if it were your own?" (1 Cor. 4:7) But we have the right to glory in all our trials, sufferings, and crosses, because the same Apostle also says: "May I never boast of anything but the cross of our Lord Jesus Christ!" (Gal. 6:14) '"

Pages such as these, taken from the *Fioretti*, reveal the spirit and language of St. Francis in all their natural charm. It was words such as these that touched people's hearts wherever he spoke, and attracted disciples just as Jesus had done in His

Gospel. We have no record of a sermon delivered by Francis, although we are sure he must have given many hundreds. Even so, we can form some idea of his manner of preaching from conversations attributed to him in the *Fioretti* with his closest disciples, Brothers Leo, Giles, Masseo, and the others. It was simple, intimate, alive, often paradoxical but always effective and convincing.

Interior life of the Order

The Penitents of Assisi, now called the *Friars Minor*, were in the process of becoming a true religious Order within the Church; in fact, one of the most active and fruitful. It is also evident from what we have said about them that this group was very different in many ways from the Orders known until then. Certainly their purpose for being was the same: the glory of God. And the essential means to attain this had not changed: love of Christ. The fundamental rules remained the same: humility, poverty, obedience, chastity. But there were many differences in the means achieving their ends.

Francis was no venerable abbot, nor did the miserable hut at Portiuncula resemble a Benedictine or Cistercian monastery. The new "monks" were often on the road, going from town to town, region to region, to preach conversion to those Christians whose practice of religion had somehow lapsed into indifference or who were already engulfed in a life of sin.

And yet in the early days of Franciscan history, certain tendencies can be discerned that would later disappear or diminish with time. There were times when Francis missed the days when he was alone and could retire to some cave or hidden refuge to devote himself to contemplation. More and more toward the end of his life he manifested a decided preference for solitude. However, he would always be equally devoted to preaching, and would continue to the end to engage in it occasionally. What he enjoyed least was the administration of his Order, and he left this to others as soon as he possibly could.

Among his earliest disciples, quite a few followed a similar evolution. Several of them — especially Brothers Silvester and Rufino, and even Giles, too, at times — began to live more and more as anchorites deep in the forests of Umbria.

At that time, the Order of the Friars Minor did not yet have a rule of life fixed once and for all, embracing all aspects of the monastic life. On the contrary, everything about it was dynamic, evolving, and responsive to the demands of the time and place.

Francis led the way in giving his brothers the example of prolonged retreats in various hermitages he had created for himself.

Let us try to understand what was going on in his mind and heart.

The dangers of preaching

Francis threw himself into preaching after hearing the Gospel on St. Matthias' feast in 1209. He was an immediate and brilliant success. We have seen how disciples gathered around him. We have related his conquest of Clare Offreduccio and the foundation of the Order of the Poor Ladies at St. Damian's. There were many other triumphs during his missions. For example, the conversion of Brother Guido Vagnotelli at Cortona, which is told in Chapter 37 of the *Fioretti*. There was the conversion in Florence of John Parenti, a doctor from the University of Bologna and the future evangelizer of Corsica, as well as a future minister general of the Order. Likewise, the conversion of Albert of Pisa, who would become a minister general, and of Agnellus, who would implant the Order in England.

But it was precisely through these victories that Francis understood the great danger inherent in preaching, which he called "dust weighing down our spiritual feet."

How could he fail to rejoice at his successes, escape the temptation to vainglory, or resist the crowds' ovations? There were times when Francis' peregrinations resembled a public triumph. When he approached a city, church bells would ring, people would throng along his path, and he would be led in a procession to the place where he was to stay. Loaves of bread were brought to him so he could bless them. He couldn't help hearing the cries that so often rose from his audiences: *"Ecco il Santo! — There's the Saint!"*

This caused concern to his closest companions. They would ask him: "Don't you hear what these people are saying?" And he usually answered that he received this veneration like the images in the churches, that is, he was no more impressed by it than the wood and stone of the paintings and statues.

But he finally realized this answer was inadequate. He tried to figure out some way to humiliate himself in response to the popular enthusiasm. Once when he was sick he ate some chicken to regain his strength. Afterwards he commanded one of the brothers to drag him through the streets on a rope, shouting to the spectators: "Look at this glutton, this worthless fellow, who ate chicken meat without telling you!"

And, as the crowds admired him all the more for his humility, he commanded another brother to shout insults at him and call him a boorish clown, good-for-nothing, useless servant, and so on. When the brother obeyed, Francis said to him with a big smile: "May God bless you, my dear brother, for what you have just said! Yes indeed, that's what the son of Pietro di Bernardone deserves to hear!"

All these tricks didn't accomplish very much and fooled no one. It was then that Francis felt strongly impelled to retire somewhere where he could be alone with his God, as he had been at the time of his conversion.

For example, we know that he spent the entire Lenten period of 1219 on an uninhabited island in Lake Trasimene. Another time, he went to a mountain hermitage at Sarteano, near Chiusi. He even withdrew to Mount Alverna where the most remarkable graces were granted him.

Solution

But even then he kept asking himself if he were really doing God's will, if he were giving his brothers the example they expected of him and to which their fidelity entitled them. He remembered the preaching life of his Jesus, and it troubled him.

Finally, he couldn't stand the uncertainty any longer. He resolved to accept the verdict of two persons whom he considered very holy: first, Brother Silvester who was living as a solitary in one of the caves of Mount Subiaso close to Assisi, on the spot where the convent of the *Carceri* now stands; and second, Clare, the Mother Abbess of St. Damian's.

Brother Silvester, alerted by Brother Masseo, immediately began to pray for divine guidance. God's answer soon came: "This is what the Lord says and what you, Brother Masseo, must tell Brother Francis: God has not called him only for his own salvation, but for the salvation of a great many souls!"

When Brother Masseo came to Abbess Clare, she told him that she—and another nun as well—had received the same answer from God as Brother Silvester.

Thereupon Brother Masseo came back to Francis who welcomed him with affection and prepared a meal for him. When Brother Masseo had finished eating, Francis led him into the neighboring forest, knelt down before him with his hands crossed on his chest, and asked: "Well, what does my Lord Jesus Christ want me to do?"

What could Masseo answer? He hastened to deliver his message. The Lord's answer was the same from Brother Silvester as from the Mother Abbess of St. Damian's: "Our Lord wants you to continue to preach, for He has not called you only for your own salvation, but for the salvation of others!"

This answer dispelled the saint's doubts. He felt as though afire with the Holy Spirit. Then he said to Brother Masseo: "Let's be on our way!"

For a while Francis devoted himself totally to missionary work, first in Italy and then in neighboring countries. However, he left the preaching in foreign lands mostly to his brothers, since Cardinal Hugolino had refused to let him go to France.

The mission of Italy

It was during this new campaign of missions that Francis gave a sermon to the birds, which has remained famous. But we shall talk about it when we discuss Francis' love for nature, as God in His goodness has created it for us.

We know that Francis went first to Rome where in 1210 the Pope had promised to grant his Order new favors when it had grown in size. And now indeed it had.

However, we know few details about this journey to Rome, except that he preached in the streets and on the public squares, and won new brothers, notably Zachary who was to become a missionary in Spain, and William, the first Englishman to become a Franciscan. It was also during this pilgrimage to Rome that Francis met an admirable woman, Lady Giacoma (or Jacqueline) Settesoli, the wife of the nobleman Gratian Frangipani.

Francis was to call this lady "his Brother Jacqueline," because of her energetic and virile nature. Five years later, in 1217, after she was widowed, she devoted herself to every kind of charitable work, under Francis' guidance.

It also seems probable that Francis asked and easily obtained from the Pope an approbation and special benediction for the mission he contemplated among the Saracens in the Middle East. However, this mission never materialized. We know that Francis did set out from an Italian seaport, but a storm cast his ship on the Dalmatian coast, which was then called Slovenia. As Francis had no way of getting to the Middle East from there, he and his companion returned to Ancona as stowaways, hiding in the hold of a ship. Needless to say, when the sailors discovered the two missionaries they spared them no insult.

As soon as Francis was back in Italy he resumed his missions, beginning with Ascoli and its environs. He was so successful there that more than thirty young men, both clerics and laymen, asked to enter the Order. During his stay in the Marches of Ancona, Francis preached at the convent of San Severino. In the audience was one of the most famous poets of that day, the troubadour William Divini, who had been honored as a poet in Rome and was widely known as "the king of verse."

Divini had come with a few of his young admirers, merely out of curiosity. At first, Francis'
sermon seemed rather dull to him. But as he went on
talking, it seemed as though arrows were darting from
Francis' heart and entering the heart of the troubadour. And yet Francis was simply propounding his
customary theme: the vanity of all things, the need
to scorn the world and to be converted in order to
escape the threatening anger of God. And when the
discourse was over, Divini was a converted man.
He came and threw himself at Francis' feet, as so
many others had done before him, and cried out:
"Brother, take me far away from men, and give me
to God!"

The very next day Francis clothed him in the
grey habit of the brothers, girded him with a cord,
and gave him the new name of "Brother Pacifico,"
because he was about to leave the world's tumult
and enter the "peace of God."

At that time and until 1220, there was no obligation to go through a year's novitiate in order to enter
the Order.

Let us not imagine, however, that Francis
gave the holy habit to every comer. He seems to have
had the gift of reading hearts.

A young nobleman discovered this in the city
of Lucca, where Francis preached next. He too had
come and thrown himself weeping at Francis' feet
after a sermon, asking him to accept him as a brother.
But Francis turned him away with unaccustomed
severity: "Your tears lie, and your heart doesn't
belong to God. Why do you want to deceive the Holy
Spirit and me, His poor servant?"

The gift of Alverna

One of the most interesting results of this
preaching campaign in Italy was the conversion of

a young knight who offered Francis his property of Mount Alverna, where the saint was to spend many fruitful days.

It was probably in 1213, and specifically on May 9th, that Francis and a companion, probably Brother Leo, were at Montefeltre in Romagna, not far from the present-day Republic of San Marino. There was a great celebration at the castle. Knights rode about on splendid mounts, pages were bustling to and fro, and there were many ladies in elegant gowns. A young nobleman was about to be knighted.

Francis did not hesitate to come forward and share in the festivities. First there was a Mass, where Francis preached. We can guess the subject of his sermon: the two knighthoods, one of this world and the other in the Lord's service. He pointed out there were two kinds of battles: those fought over worldly goods, and those waged over eternal Beauty between the angels and devils.

In any event, we know that Francis' words touched the heart of a young count, Roland of Cattani, who owned the citadel of Chiusi. After the ceremonies, he came up to Francis and said, as so many others had before him: "Father, I should like to talk with you about my salvation!"

To Roland's great surprise, Francis seemed in no hurry to talk with him. Wanting to give the young knight time to reflect on his decision, he simply said: "My son, first go and take part in the festivities of the banquet with all your friends, and then we'll talk about it at our leisure."

So the festivities went on. According to custom, there was a brilliant tournament. Afterwards the young count returned to converse with Francis. Before leaving, he said: "I own a mountain in Tuscany that is called Alverna, very secluded and isolated. It would be conducive to recollection. In case you

and your brothers want to settle there, I'll be delighted to offer it to you as a gift for the salvation
of my soul."

Now this offer seemed Providence's answer
to one of Francis' keenest and most persistent hopes.
He thanked God inwardly for this offer, and answered
Count Roland: "Lord Count, when you return to
your castle, I shall send two of my brothers to you,
so you can show them the mountain. If it is indeed
appropriate for contemplation and prayer, I shall
accept your generous offer with great joy."

It was in this way that Francis and his brothers
became not the owners—for their resolve of poverty
forbade it—but the users of Mount Alverna, where
Francis was to spend some of the most sublime hours
of his life.

APPROBATION OF THE ORDER – THE RULES

At the Lateran Council

We have already mentioned that
the rapidly growing Order convened
its first General Chapter at
Portiuncula on the feast of Pentecost,
1214. The matter of approbation had
become a pressing problem.
The verbal approbation of 1210 had
sufficed until then, but it needed
to be confirmed and expanded, and
given official form.

Now very serious obstacles seemed
to prevent such an approbation. As
we have seen, the Pope's advisers
had formulated a number of objections to it in 1210, when the question
arose of permitting Francis and
his followers to preach. The
Lateran Council which met in 1215
showed itself no less opposed to
the approbation of the two new
Orders requesting acceptance by
the Church.

The Lateran Council was very
imposing indeed. Present were at

least 400 bishops and 800 abbots or priors, as well as representatives of the Emperor of Germany, the Latin Emperor of Constantinople, the Kings of France, England, Hungary, Jerusalem, Cyprus, Aragon, and many Lombard city-states. Convoked in April, 1215, it opened on November 11, in the Basilica of St. John Lateran. We do not have the records of the acts passed by this Council, but only its 70 Canons or *Capitula*.

It was there that Francis of Assisi first met the Spaniard Dominic de Guzman, founder of the Friars Preachers. They were immediately in complete sympathy, and had no trouble recognizing their perfect fraternity of intentions and methods, despite certain obvious differences.

Both Orders were on the point of being approved by the Church. They were at the same stage of development, that of temporary, oral approbation. They were both waiting to see what the Council would decide for each of them.

As for the Council's agenda, we know that Pope Innocent III, at whose request it had convened, again made a very pressing appeal for a crusade. Francis, who had his own ideas about the subject, was to respond to the Pontiff's call. We know how deeply the salvation of the infidels concerned Francis. As he saw it, the real crusade was not the one by conquerors with swords, but the one by missionaries ready to shed their blood for the Christian faith.

But the Pope also spoke very forcefully of the need for reform within the Church. He discussed the threats to the faith inherent in the new heresies, those of the Waldensians and the Cathari (or Albigensians). The first canons of the Lateran Council were followed by many others on the proper administration of the sacraments. The question of the religious Orders was settled by Canons 12 and 13.

At first glance, the Council's decision on the Orders seemed entirely negative. The Council found there were already enough convents of all kinds, and that a number of them needed to be roused from their somnolent state. The Council therefore ordered the convening of provincial chapters every three years, but remained resolutely hostile to the creation of new Orders.

However, the canon devoted to this problem and that expressed the views of the bishops with a view to restricting the number of new forms of religious life, was not directed against the new institutes of Francis and Dominic. In fact, both of these founders would soon receive formal approbation by the Holy See.

What really happened? It is logical to conclude that the Pope used his authority to allow the two new Orders to give more conclusive proof of their worth. Both Orders had already achieved considerable results and public acclaim. So the Council's condemnation of new Orders was, in a sense, put in abeyance as far as the Friars Minor and the Friars Preachers were concerned. They remained under the protection of the Holy Father. They would be allowed to develop as much as God permitted, and the day might soon come when they would be given definitive approbation by the Church's highest authorities.

A text of that epoch provides us proof both of the edifying life of the Friars Minor and the solicitude shown for them by the Papal Court.

An eloquent text of 1216

Right after the Council, Francis was able to bring his daughter Clare, Abbess of St. Damian's, a special papal benediction granting her what she had asked so insistently: "the privilege of poverty."

Giotto   *Church of St. Francis of Assisi*   *1296-1299*

St. Francis renounces his paternal heritage.

Giotto   Church of St. Francis of Assisi   1296-1299

St. Francis gives his cloak to a beggar.

Giotto   *Life of St. Francis of Assisi*   *1296-1299*

The sermon to the birds.

Giotto

St. Francis driving the demons from Arezzo.

Veneziano

The stigmatization of St. Francis

Giotto   Bardi C.S. Croce

The death of St. Francis

Giotto

Friar kissing the hand of St. Francis (detail).

Giotto   Florence S. Croce

Burial of St. Francis (detail).

In 1216 the Papal Court had been established in Perugia. In October of the same year, a French prelate, Jacques de Vitry, passed through Perugia on his way from the Holy Land. One of his letters, written to a friend in Genoa, has come down to us. It reads in part as follows:

"During my stay at the Papal Court, I saw many things that greatly saddened me. Everybody was so preoccupied with temporal and worldly matters, with politics, juridical questions, that I hardly had a chance to speak or hear anyone else speak of spiritual things!

"However, one thing greatly consoled me in this locality. A large number of persons of both sexes, including many noblemen and persons of wealth, have abandoned all things for the love of Christ and renounced the world. They are now called 'Friars Minor.' I must say, the Pope and cardinals hold them in high esteem. And they work unceasingly to save souls from the vanities of the world, so they may not perish. Already the grace of God has allowed them to reap abundant harvests....

"They live after the model of the primitive Christian community, of which it is written: 'The community of believers were of one heart and one mind' (Acts 4:32). During the day they go into the towns and villages to fish for souls. At night they return to solitary places where they devote themselves to prayer. The women live together in various refuges on the outskirts of the towns. They refuse to accept alms and want to live only by the work of their hands....

"As for the men of this new Order, they assemble once a year at a given place, to eat in common and rejoice in the Lord. And there, in the presence of honest folk, they discuss and establish laws that the Pope later consecrates by his approbation. Afterwards, they disperse and go out for the entire year through Lombardy and Tuscany, into Apulia and Sicily. Quite recently, a holy and God-fearing man named Nicholas, who was the Pope's confessor, abandoned the Curia to seek refuge among these Brothers Minor. But the Pope couldn't spare him, and soon called him back."

Such a text reveals the favor with which the Franciscan Order was held by the Supreme Pontiff. Evidently, this favor had not ended with the death of Innocent III, for his successor, Honorius III — who had been Pope three months (July, 1216) when Jacques de Vitry was writing — was precisely the one who wanted to know the decisions of the Franciscan chapter, so he too could approve them, as his predecessor had done.

As for the Pope's confessor, we know he was Nicholas Chiaramonti, Bishop of Tusculum. Soon after Jacques de Vitry's letter was written, he was made a cardinal, and became one of the great friends of the Franciscan Order.

Cardinal Hugolino

But the principal protector of Francis and his followers was already another dignitary of the Church, Cardinal Hugolino. His influence on the newly-formed Order has been sharply criticized by Sabatier, who did not understand it and accused the Cardinal of having vitiated Francis' inspiration. To the contrary, it is generally admitted today that the beneficent influence of the Order on the whole Church, by encouraging spiritual reform and a return to the spirit of the Gospel, was exercised chiefly through the close friendship Francis and Clare enjoyed with Cardinal Hugolino.

Who was this man? He was to become Pope, and a very great Pope, from 1227 to 1241. He belonged to the family of the Counts of Segni, which was also the family of Innocent III, and a little later of Alexander IV. It has often been claimed he was born between 1140 and 1145, which would have made him about fifteen or twenty years older than his uncle Innocent III, and then he would have died at the age of 96 or even 101! Actually, he was probably born at Agnani, about 1170. Innocent III made him a cardinal in 1198, shortly after becoming Pope. Hugolino's influence continued to grow with the years. Honorius III in turn placed his trust in him.

Cardinal Hugolino was endowed with great intelligence and was attentive to what we call "the signs of the times." He had understood the extraordinary timeliness of the new Orders in the Church. The Friars Preachers had already fought so well against the tragic errors of the Albigensians (or Cathari). The Friars Minor alone, he felt, were capable of fighting effectively against the very dangerous movement of the Poor Men of Lyons, or Waldensians.

Although Hugolino had often, perhaps too often, been used by the Popes on political missions and entrusted with various legations, he was inclined to limit himself increasingly to religious activities. He had recognized in the mendicant brothers the messengers of true reform within the Church. But he knew it was necessary to guide their steps, to prevent them from falling into false mysticism, to keep them in pure orthodoxy, and hence to extend to them a constant, enlightened, and efficacious friendship.

As for the Franciscan Order, it is certain Cardinal Hugolino was immensely attracted to its evangelical spirit. In fact he had adopted in his own life the fundamental principle of imitating Christ in His poverty as far as possible, and he had seen the great benefit the apostolic spirit could be to the Church.

We have already spoken of the influence Cardinal Hugolino exerted on the Poor Clares. He could have been considered to be their second founder, he had done so much to encourage and protect them.

He would even be one of the most energetic propagators of the Franciscan "Third Order," to which we shall devote an entire chapter later in the book.

We should point out at once that after Francis' death it was he who entrusted to Thomas of Celano the mission of writing the first biography of Francis, and who, as Pope, insisted on canonizing the founder of the Friars Minor two short years after his death.

It was he who laid the first stone of the sepulcher church of Assisi in honor of the saint. But, on the other hand, he was careful to point out in a special Bull (*Quo elongati*, 1230), that the *Testament* of Francis had no power to obligate. This was to have a significant influence on the great debate among the "Spirituals" over Francis' successor.

So we see that Cardinal Hugolino has undeniable rights to the gratitude of the entire Order and of the whole Church that was to benefit so richly from Franciscan activities.

There are those, including Bastianini, who hold that it was at his residence in Rome, during the Lateran Council of 1215, that Francis and Dominic became better acquainted and established a very holy friendship.

We do not know the exact facts of the matter. It is possible that the close friendship between Hugolino and Francis began only during the pontificate of Honorius III, about the year 1216. We are certain, however, that the Cardinal, accompanied by a large retinue of clerics and men-at-arms, went from Perugia to visit the brothers when they were assembled at Portiuncula.

Once there, he wanted to see with his own eyes how they lived. When he discovered they ate on the bare earth and slept on straw, we are told he was so deeply moved that he broke into tears and cried out: "What fate does God have in store for those of us who live continually in luxury and comfort?"

From that time on, contacts between the Papal Court and Portiuncula became more and more frequent. It was about this time, some claim, that Pope Honorius III granted the famous Portiuncula Indulgence. But it is very possible this Indulgence dates from the end of the thirteenth century.

The following account has come down to us of a remarkable episode in the relations between Cardinal Hugolino and Francis.

There were now so many brothers that Francis wanted to see them set out to conquer souls all over the world, and first of all in Germany, Hungary, France, Spain, and the Holy Land. Francis chose France as the theater of his own missionary activities.

On the way to France, he passed through Florence. He learned that Cardinal Hugolino was there as papal legate, to bring peace among the cities and preach the crusade. Francis immediately went to see him. The Cardinal received him with great joy and asked him about his plans. When he heard Francis was about to leave Italy, he told him in no uncertain terms: "Brother Francis, I do not want you to go beyond the Alps. There are several prelates at the Papal Court who are ill-disposed toward you and your brothers. The other cardinals who, like myself, are for you will not have as much authority to defend you if you go too far afield."

"But how can I send my brothers out on missions if I don't go myself?" Francis asked.

The Cardinal would not accept this as a valid reason and insisted that Francis proceed no farther. Francis obeyed and sent another brother to France, the one known as Brother Pacifico, the former troubadour he had converted.

Hugolino and the Franciscan Rule

A man like Hugolino was too well informed not to realize that the fluid and hazy nature of the Order's institutions could impede its growth unless something were done to give them more concrete form. There was a Rule of course, but it consisted entirely of texts from the Gospel, without any specific regulations for the daily living and interior organization of the Order.

It is probable that the Cardinal advised Francis to prepare a clearly defined Rule. Meanwhile, he personally assumed the responsibility for providing a Rule for the *Poor Ladies* of St. Damian's. The nuns who would later be known as the *Poor Clares* were beginning to branch out into various dioceses, and a Constitution was needed. One difficulty arose from the fact that the Lateran Council had prohibited the creation of new Orders. This obstacle could be overcome only by adapting to a Rule already approved by the Church. We know, for example, that the Dominicans were invited to choose a Rule among those already in operation, and that they chose the Rule of the Premonstratensians, based on the Rule of St. Augustine.

For the Poor Clares, Cardinal Hugolino chose the Benedictine Rule as his model. But we have already pointed out that neither Clare nor Francis felt the provisions of this Rule gave sufficient importance to what they considered the most necessary: "the privilege of poverty." But this was to be clarified later on.

We can well believe the Cardinal urged Francis to get on with his work.

It is certain that in order to devote himself to this major task, Francis resigned as the director of the Order. In 1220, the role of governing the Order was entrusted to Peter Catani as its Vicar General, and after his death the following year, to Brother Elias.

The title of Vicar General would seem to indicate that Francis was still the true head in the eyes of all the brothers. In any case, he certainly considered himself the Order's head, and as such set about writing what has been called "the first Rule." He was aided in this very sensitive task by an experienced brother, Caesar of Speyer.

How was this work done? Obviously, Francis and Caesar had to build first of all on what had been enacted at Rivo-Torto in 1210, since this is what Pope Innocent III had orally approved. But since then the Order had engaged in a number of experiments. A few brothers had lived as hermits. Most of the others had been sent on missions to various places, either in Italy or in the neighboring kingdoms. At the very time Caesar of Speyer was serving as Francis' secretary in preparing the new Rule, he had just been charged by the Order's Chapter General to lead an important mission of the brothers in Germany.

Caesar, therefore, sent his mission companions on ahead, telling them to wait for him in Lombardy. Meanwhile, he remained either at Spoleto or at the *Carceri*, a solitude close to Assisi, to work with Francis on the Rule.

For the past ten years, Francis had continually sent short *Admonitions* to his brothers, both for those who lived as hermits and those on missions. A number of these *Counsels* have come down to us.

They were also taken into consideration in the writing of the 1221 Rule.

It seems, however, that this Rule was never written down in final form, and that it was never considered as the Rule of the Order. The proof of this is that shortly after the preparation of this rough draft, a new Rule, the so-called Rule of 1223, was written, and it was approved by the Holy See.

Caesar of Speyer had left for Germany in September, 1221. The new Rule, composed by Francis, received the approbation of Pope Honorius III only through the Bull *Solet annuere*, dated November 29, 1223. During the two intervening years, it seems a whole series of discussions were held within the Order, and probably also with outside authorities, concerning the Constitution Francis had worked out.

Cardinal Hugolino certainly lent his support to these efforts, since he was a great friend of the Order. But he also believed the Rule should not be given a definitive form that would make it impracticable in later times for the ordinary run of men and women. He felt the nature of the Order lent itself to the mitigations he wanted to introduce in the practice of perfect poverty. Brother Elias, whom Francis had just appointed as his Vicar General, was among those who feared Francis was going too far. And while Hugolino approved Brother Elias' more moderate position, he wanted to serve as a mediator in the debate.

The problem of higher learning

To get an idea of the serious differences that would arise, we must situate the developing Order in the general history of the Church at the start of the thirteenth century. It was the time when the great Catholic universities were coming into being, and first among them the University of Paris, which would soon outrank all others in the Christian world. Now Francis was no enemy of higher learning, but he had grown up outside this new movement. He did not realize its breadth and fruitfulness. It would certainly be unfair to say he was against theological science, but he just didn't think it was meant for his "Lesser" brothers.

We have a very explicit *Admonition* of his on the subject. According to Celano, he once said: "We must honor and esteem very highly all theologians and others who help us by explaining God's Word to us, for they give us the spirit and the life."

As for himself and his brothers, he believed they should limit themselves to moral and religious preaching of a very practical sort, without getting lost in deep questions of dogma.

But everyone in the Order didn't agree with this view. The same problem had arisen among the Dominicans, and they had solved it as early as 1219 by creating a "school of theology" at Bologna, then a very famous university center.

Inevitably, there were some Friars Minor eager to do the same thing, especially in view of the fact that their ranks included more than one doctor from the University of Bologna.

In fact, about this time Brother Peter of Stacia inaugurated a sort of Franciscan school of theology in the city of Bologna.

We should now call to mind one of the most serious objections that had been raised in the entourage of Innocent III at the first request for authorization in 1210. Certain cardinals had said: "They want to preach, but in order to preach one must first study; and to study one must have houses where this study can be pursued. It is therefore impossible to found an Order *that will have absolutely no possessions!*"

Was Clare's beloved "privilege of poverty," was Francis' great dream for his Order incompatible with advanced study, with theological science? Here we have the whole drama that was unfolding in Francis' conscience at the time he was writing the definitive Rule for his Order: *he had to choose between poverty and learning.*

He either had to choose poverty, and then his Order would be doomed to theological ignorance, or he would have to insist that his followers acquire theological science, and then he would have to renounce perfect poverty!

It is hard for us to realize how spirited the debates were over these alternatives, not only in the Franciscan Order, but everywhere in Christendom. A workable solution had to be found, and of course it was. Forty years later, all these arguments were already forgotten. It is enough to mention only Bonaventure, who became one of Francis' successors as head of the Order and who, after Celano, was Francis' first biographer. He was a theologian of the first rank, and established his residence not at Portiuncula but at Paris, near the greatest University in the world at that time.

Love of poverty

But Francis never stopped fighting throughout his life to maintain the principle of poverty in his Order. On his side were many brothers, especially the older ones and those who had been won over by his words in the very beginning.

A few facts will help us to understand his spirit during this period of heated discussions over the definitive Rule he wanted to establish.

At first he was very much opposed to the school of theology founded by Peter of Stacia at Bologna. In the name of obedience, he commanded all the brothers in the house to leave. Even one of them who was sick in bed had to be carried out with the others. They all complied, with the exception of Peter of Stacia. And Francis, for all his meekness, is said to have cursed Peter.

Francis could not understand why the brothers should acquire these large and costly books, without which it was literally impossible for them to pursue their studies. Certain explicit words of Francis on this occasion have been recorded. He reminded them that when Christ had sent out His apostles, He had told them to take nothing with them for the journey, and added his own commentary: "I understand these words to mean that the brothers must have nothing of their own: only the habit and cord, pants, and sandals, in such instances when these are all indispensable."

One day, one of the ministers asked him: "What must I do, since I have volumes worth 50 silver pounds?" That was the price of certain works in those days. In our current money, these 50 pounds would be equivalent to more than $800.00 in American money (1958 rate of exchange).

Francis answered: "As for me, I wouldn't want the ownership of such books to make me disobey the Gospel, according to which I have pledged myself to live."

We can therefore understand that he included the following provision in his Rule, concerning the minister general of the Order: "And the perfect General must not be a collector of books!"

Inevitably friction developed between Francis and those humble and very devout brothers such as Brother Leo and many others on the one hand, and the other brothers already engaged in higher learning before they entered the Order and who felt they had the Cardinal's support. In any event, Francis never ceased reminding all the brothers of his primitive ideal.

On one occasion when Cardinal Hugolino discreetly made a few remarks concerning the value of books and learning, Francis silently took him by the hand and led him into the midst of the brothers. Then he said in a very loud voice:

"My brothers, my brothers, the Lord has called me to walk in the paths of humility and simplicity, and with me He has called all those who want to follow and imitate me. Therefore, by way of a Rule, let there be no talk of the Rule of St. Benedict or any others! For the Lord has told me He wanted me to be simple-minded and foolish, such as no one had ever seen, and that it was His intention to lead me and all my brothers along with me by other paths than those of science. And God will shame you, with all your wisdom and your learning! I foresee He will send you executors of His punishments and chastise you in such a way that you will be forced to return to your true condition, to your own great loss!"

It is evident that what Francis feared about science and knowledge was the pride he saw springing up in those who were trying to acquire it.

He had the highest esteem for the friends of prayer, the hermits of his Order, and for the lowliest missionaries ready to give their lives for the Faith. To his mind, these were truly his "Knights of the Round Table."

It is very inspiring to observe throughout Francis' life his burning desire to resemble Jesus and to imitate Him in His poverty, in a world where money has always ruled.

We must admit, however, that certain fears were coming to light around him. In the end, the definitive Rule of the Order, the Rule of 1223, was to a degree a *compromise* between opposing tendencies, as we shall soon see.

The Rule of 1223

In 1221, Francis had been helped by Brother Caesar of Speyer, but in 1223 he had a collaborator who wielded far greater authority in the Church — Cardinal Hugolino in person. We imagine their co-operation was along the following lines: First, Francis would meditate and pray. Then he would tell the Cardinal what several of the brothers, including the most enlightened and experienced, had recommended — especially Brother Elias, whom Francis had named Vicar General of the Order. The Cardinal would listen to the saint's inspirations with great deference, but would translate, interpret, and mitigate them, and thus bring them into closer conformity with what he considered "permanent human capacities." He distrusted the enthusiasms of a generation that would saddle future generations with a yoke they might find intolerable.

Here is an example.

Francis wanted to insert the following article into the Rule: "When the ministers are not careful to see that the brothers observe the Rule in all its rigor, *permission shall be granted to the brothers to follow this same Rule against the ministers' wishes.*"

This meant that the mitigations authorized by the superiors could be rejected by the brothers who so decided. The Rule was placed above the decisions of the local superiors.

This surely had to do with the problems already mentioned within the Order: the matter of *higher learning* versus *absolute poverty.* Cardinal Hugolino discerned in this text a source of dissension within the Order. He said so to Francis, but the latter insisted that the disputed article be included in the Rule.

"Well then!" the Cardinal said very simply, "I'll see to it that the sense of the thing is preserved, and that only its expression is modified."

Francis agreed, but the Cardinal's draft left only a very weakened version of Francis' initial idea:

"And if certain brothers know and acknowledge that it is impossible for them to observe the Rule in spirit, they may and should have recourse to their ministers. And these will receive them with kindness and charity and treat them in such a way that their words and acts are those of a servant toward his masters. For it is fitting that the ministers be servants of all the brothers."

This meant the Rule was to remain unchanged, but that the ministers could dispense from it. Yes, but it didn't express what Francis had in mind. The same thing very probably occurred throughout the drafting of the Rule. Francis could see that what he proposed was being modified in the sense of a mitigation that he had not wanted to provide but that the Cardinal had deemed necessary.

One of the points about which Francis must have been most sensitive was the total absence from the definitive text of the Rule of all the Gospel texts that he had made the sole content of his first Rule of 1210. We can readily understand what was going on within him when we read in an ancient text on the origins of the Order, *The Mirror of Perfection*, the following passage:

"Francis wanted to have several things inscribed in the Rule that God had revealed to him in prayer and meditation as destined to be useful to the Order. But when he would express these things to the brothers, the latter judged them to be too burdensome and impracticable.... And he for his part didn't want to argue with them...."

For instance, there were the words that had struck Francis so powerfully in 1209, from the Gospel of St. Matthias: "Do not carry a walking staff or traveling bag; wear no sandals and greet no one along the way" (Lk. 10:4). In his *Second Biography*, Thomas of Celano says: "He had wanted to insert these words into the Rule, but in the final draft they were omitted."

We can have no doubt, therefore, that great arguments raged around Francis at the time the Rule of 1223 was written, and that Brother Elias led the group of "objectors." According to one early source, he came to tell Francis, who had secluded himself from everyone in a mountain cave: "The ministers of Italy have learned that you were writing a new Rule, and now they have come to warn you that you must write a Rule they can observe; because if you don't do that, they will refuse to accept your Rule and you will have written it for yourself alone and not for them!"

What is the truth of the matter? Everybody agrees that the Rule approved by Pope Honorius III on November 29, 1223, expressed the Franciscan character in an eminent way. If our sources did not tell us about the many battles over its drafting, no one would guess it wasn't exactly what Francis had intended. So we see that Hugolino had carefully safeguarded the essentials.

Besides, Francis accepted authorship of the Rule, as we see in the Prologue, which contained the following words in Latin: "Brother Francis promises obedience and reverence to the Lord Pope Honorius...and the other brothers must be required to obey Brother Francis."

So it was indeed in Francis' name that the Rule was presented to the Sovereign Pontiff.

In addition, we find in the Rule of 1223 all the principles that molded Francis' life. Right after the Prologue, the Rule commands the brothers to live according to the Gospel, in obedience, poverty, and chastity. After that come twelve chapters that constitute the Rule in the strict sense—twelve chapters in honor of the twelve apostles, most probably. And these chapters are in the purest Franciscan spirit: express prohibition to accept any money whatsoever (Chapter 4), or to possess anything whatever (Chapter 6); the command to work (Chapter 5), and to beg without shame when necessary (also Chapter 6); the command to wear only poor clothing, but without taking pride in poverty or condemning those who are better clothed (Chapter 7); the need for the brothers during their missions through the world to show themselves gentle, modest, peaceful, humble, and affectionate to all, to avoid all quarreling, not to judge or condemn anyone, and to bring "peace" to every house they enter, according to the evangelical words: "Peace to this house!"; and finally to eat whatever they are offered (Chapter 3); the prohibition to enter a nuns' convent (Chapter 11) or to preach without the authorization of the local bishop (Chapter 6); the obligation for friar priests to recite the Roman Office and for lay members to recite the office of the Our Fathers (Chapter 3).

The spirit of St. Francis is very well summed up in Chapter 6 of the Rule:

"The brothers must pass through the world like pilgrims and strangers, without possessing anything on earth but the indestructible treasure of most high poverty."

The whole of Francis' legacy is contained in these words. And it has come down to us because the Franciscan Order has remained, in all its branches which were henceforth to be integrally united in spirit, one of the most vitally alive Orders of the entire Church.

MISSIONS TO THE INFIDELS

One of Francis' fondest hopes

Even in their failures the saints
deserve our admiration. We see this
clearly in Francis of Assisi's various
efforts to bring the Gospel to the
Moslems, or infidels as they were
called. He made several attempts to
go to the Middle East himself, and
succeeded only once. He sent several
of his disciples to Morocco. On every
count he failed. His missionary
forays have left no tangible results.
And yet we are delighted with his
zeal and perseverance, his eagerness
to give his life, his blood, indeed
his whole being for his Savior and
for the salvation of souls. We know
beyond a doubt that even these
unsuccessful ventures have left us
an example, an impetus that has
become part and parcel of the
heritage he bequeathed not only
to the Friars Minor but to the whole
Church. In particular, they probably

fired the crusading desires of St. Louis, King of France.

We need only mention in passing Francis' abortive mission to the Middle East in 1212. His ship was cast on the shores of Slovenia, as we remember, and he was obliged to return to Italy by way of Ancona.

A second expedition a short while later likewise met with failure.

We shall now follow in greater detail the more important efforts, which were resolved upon at the famous Chapter of 1219, presided over by Cardinal Hugolino, Protector of the Order.

Toward Tunis and Morocco

The mission to Tunis quickly came to an end. Brothers Giles and Eliu had been sent there. But hardly had they disembarked and begun to make known their plan to preach the Gospel, when the few Christians living in the Tunisian Regency took fright. They were convinced the missionaries would provoke an explosion of fanaticism among the Moslems, and they would be its first victims. So they tried to persuade the brothers to re-embark as fast as possible. As the zealous missioners refused, the Tunisian Christians took them by force and sent them back to Italy by boat. Only Brother Eliu, one of the leaders of the mission band, managed to escape and remain in Tunisia, where, as we might have expected, he soon suffered martyrdom.

He died an admirable death. Holding the Rule of his Order in his joined hands, he knelt and begged forgiveness publicly for all the sins he might have committed since his entrance into the Friars Minor. And in this posture he met his death by decapitation.

The mission to Morocco ended in similar fashion. The sultan of that land used to be called the miramolin. We know the names of the brothers who were sent to this Moslem prince: Vito, Berard, Peter, Adjuto, Accursorio and Otto.

As they were leaving, Francis gave them his last admonitions and bade them farewell with great emotion.

There is an early account that cites the following words as those he spoke on that occasion:

"My dear sons, God has commanded me to send you to the land of the Saracens to announce the Faith, to proclaim it, and to fight the law of Mohammed.... Be ready, therefore, to do the will of God!"

"Father," the missioners answered as one, "we are ready to obey you in all things!"

"My very dear sons," Francis continued, "in order that you may carry out God's command more perfectly, be vigilant always to maintain peace among yourselves, union, and an unquenchable love. Do not envy anyone, for it was through envy that original sin came. Be patient in suffering, and humble amid success! Imitate Christ in poverty, obedience, and chastity. For our Lord Jesus Christ was born poor. He lived the life of a poor man. He taught poverty and He died poor. And to show us how much He loved chastity, he chose to be born of a Virgin Mother. He preserved the virginal state Himself, He died surrounded by virgins, and He taught us to live this virginal state. And finally, He was obedient from His birth until His death on the cross. Put your trust in God alone. It is He who guides and protects us. Always carry your Rule and your Breviary on your persons, and never fail to recite all the divine offices of the day. All of you, obey your Brother Vito. O my sons, in very truth I rejoice over your good will although my heart bleeds at the thought of having to be separated from you. But that doesn't matter. God's will must come before our own. And so I beg you always to keep the Lord's sufferings before your eyes, so that this spectacle may strengthen you and encourage you to suffer for Him in your turn...."

While this discourse is not rigorously histor-ical, it certainly gives excellent expression to Fran-cis´ habitual sentiments and reproduces the thoughts that were the fabric of his talks to his brothers.

The brothers being sent to Morocco declared they were ready to do everything their Father had counseled.

Then our six missioners were on their way. They passed through Aragon, where their leader Vito fell sick and had to be left behind. Then they went through Castille and Portugal. They were only five when they arrived in Seville, in the land of the Moslems, where they were arrested and led before the authorities of the city.

They declared they were on their way to see the miramolin. And so it was decided to send them to him, for Seville was then a Moslem city.

The miramolin at that time was Abu-Jacob, who was no bitter enemy of Christians. After his father was severely defeated in Spain in 1212, he lost all hope of conquering the Christians. The son had even taken a Christian prince into his serv-ice and placed him at the head of his army. This was the Infante Dom Pedro of Portugal, who had quarreled with his brother, the King of Portugal.

So when the five Franciscan brothers were presented to the miramolin and made their inten-tions known to him, his first reaction was to give them complete freedom to preach as they pleased. He even decided they should be billeted at the residence of Dom Pedro, their fellow Christian.

On their journey, the brothers had learned a little Arabic. Their leader was now Brother Berard. Taking advantage of the permission granted to them, our missioners began to preach in the streets and in the public squares. Quite probably, their words aroused greater aversion than sympathy. One day when the miramolin was returning from a visit to the tombs of his ancestors, he came upon them as Brother Berard stood in a cart preaching. Abu-Jacob, no doubt pressed by his people, put an end to the preaching. But he did it in a very moderate way, for he limited himself to demanding that the brothers be sent back to Christian lands, without suffering any harm.

Dom Pedro was charged with executing the sentence. He put them on a boat going to Ceuta, and told them to return to Italy.

Now, our missionaries were not willing to go home. They had received a command to preach in Morocco, and they had no intention of desisting.

With courageous obstinacy, they seized the first chance to return to Morocco and resume their preaching.

From that moment on, their life in Morocco was a game of wits between themselves and the authorities. Now it was the miramolin who had them arrested, and again it was Pedro who would stop them in the middle of a sermon and send them back to Ceuta or into some area of the interior under careful surveillance to keep them from accomplishing their mission.

Now Friday, we know, is for the Moslems the equivalent of the Christians' Sunday. One Friday, therefore, when the missioners had once more slipped by their guards, they began preaching on a public square where they knew the miramolin would soon pass. This time, the prince's patience was worn too thin. Violently angry, he had the brothers arrested. They were stripped naked and rolled on broken glass, then subjected to an interrogation like those of the first Christians before the pagan judges. Their answers threw Abu-Jacob into such an uncontrollable rage that he rushed at them and decapitated all five of them with his own hands.

Dom Pedro realized they were true martyrs. He reverently gathered up their remains and had them transported to Coïmbra in Portugal. Queen Urraca came personally to welcome the martyred bodies amid a vast crowd. At her command the relics of the five Franciscan martyrs were placed in the Church of the Holy Cross in Coïmbra.

The account of the deaths of these five martyrs soon spread throughout the Christian world. Their martyrdom had occurred on January 16, 1220. Among the witnesses to their glorification at Coïmbra was a young Augustinian canon, named Anthony. This young man of twenty-five was so inspired by the example of the five martyrs that he in turn yearned to be immolated for the Gospel. He went to Morocco, where he fell ill, and then was cast on the shores of Sicily. From there he went to Portiuncula to request admission into the Order. He was to be famous for his zeal, his eloquence and his learning. He died in 1231, when only thirty-six years old. In 1232, just eleven months after his death, Gregory IX canonized him. This was St. Anthony of Padua.

It is said that when Francis listened to the account of his brothers' martyrdom read at the Chapter of Pentecost, 1221, he felt such joy that he cried out: "Now I can say in very truth that I have five real brothers!"

We can surmise that he envied their fate a little, because he too had tried his luck, if we may say so. He had gone into infidel lands to shed his blood, but had failed to achieve his purpose.

Francis' crusade

The so-called "Crusade of St. Francis" took place in 1219. A very early text gives us two principles which guided Francis' thinking on crusades. The first, probably never put into practice in his own time, was to be used by Charles de Foucauld in our own era:

"Do not argue with unbelievers, but be humbly subject to all creatures for the love of God, and thus bear witness to what Christianity really is."

The second principle was the one the brothers used in Morocco: "Announce God's Word to the infidels, teach them about the Blessed Trinity, encourage them to believe in It and to receive holy Baptism so they can become Christians.... Always have before your eyes Christ's words: 'He who loses his life for my sake, will receive eternal life.'"

For Francis, therefore, a crusade certainly was not a war with arms against the Moslems. He didn't totally condemn the crusades which had been understood in this spirit since Urban II. But he was shocked by the abuses the Crusaders too often committed, thus giving the infidels a false notion of the Christian Faith.

Francis was buoyed by high hopes when he set out for the Middle East for a third time. With him was Peter Catani. Very probably, they were accompanied by many more companions.

In any event, on June 24, 1219, the Feast of St. John, Francis and Peter Catani set out from Ancona, and went straight toward the Holy Land, where the Christians still held the imposing fortress of St. John of Acre.

They were welcomed by Brother Elias, who had gone on before them. It was decided that Francis and his brothers would join the army of the Crusaders who, since March, 1218, had been besieging the city of Damietta in Egypt under the leadership of John de Brienne.

It was a hard-fought war, and the Christians had made very little headway. Before attempting to approach the Moslem leaders, Francis felt he must first preach to the Christians behavior that would do greater honor to their religion. When he arrived, several assaults against Damietta had been repulsed and the Crusaders were suffering heavy losses. They were deeply discouraged. This made them far more receptive to the saint's preaching than if they had been in the flush of victory.

We have most reliable testimony on Francis' influence from Jacques de Vitry, who wrote as follows from Damietta to his friends in France.

"Regnier, the prior of St. Michael's at St. John of Acre, has just entered the Order of the Friars Minor. Indeed, the Order is propagating itself throughout the world. This proves that it reproduces in exact detail the life of the first Christian communities and even that of the Apostles.... Likewise, my own cleric, the Englishman Collins, and two more of my companions have entered this Order, namely, Master Michael and Sir Matthew, to whom I had entrusted the parish of the Holy Cross at St. John of Acre. I'm having a very hard time keeping my precentor, and Henry and the others from doing the same!"

So we see there was a veritable infatuation for the Order at the sight of Francis and his brothers. And we surmise that Francis' sermons in the Christian camp at Damietta must have drawn large crowds.

A visit to the Soldan

And yet that was not why Francis had come to Egypt. His own "crusade," as he understood it, was to present himself unarmed to the leader of the infidels and proclaim the Gospel to him.

Accompanied by a single brother, whose name was Illuminato, according to Bonaventure's account, he proceeded to the Saracen outposts. The two men were immediately stopped, and even maltreated. But as Francis kept shouting: "Soldan! Soldan!" they understood he was asking to be led to the leader of the True Believers. Once in the presence of Malik-al-Kamil, Francis talked to him of God, of Jesus Christ, and of the Christian Faith. There was something so touching about his demeanor that the Soldan was not angry with him. And yet they could not communicate very well, since Francis didn't know the language of the infidels. The Soldan, for his part, simply said to Francis: "Pray for me that God may reveal to me the religion that is most pleasing to Him."

According to Jacques de Vitry, Francis was allowed to preach for several days in the Mohammedan camp. But his efforts were without success. It is thought the Soldan had given Francis a safe-conduct or some sign so that no one would harm him. As we remember, the miramolin in Morocco had started out much the same way.

In any event, Francis' stay among the Moslems could not last very long. He was driven back to Damietta. On November 5, 1219, the city had fallen to the Crusaders. This capture had been accompanied by frightful pillage and such revolting actions that Francis felt he could not remain any longer among Christians who had proved themselves so unworthy of the Gospel of Christ.

In Palestine

Needless to say, Francis refused to return to Italy without making another try at missionary activity. He therefore decided to return to Palestine, and first of all to St. John of Acre.

The saint's biographers are unanimous in their view that he wanted to make a pilgrimage to all the places sanctified by Christ's earthly presence. That was what most unarmed Christians visiting Palestine did. St. Louis, King of France, a little later, would not be prevented from going to Jerusalem with a safe-conduct because he was told it would be unworthy of a king of France to enter Jerusalem except as a conqueror of infidels. So it was not too difficult to obtain permission to visit the Holy Places under predetermined conditions.

It seems quite evident that Francis took advantage of this opportunity. His whole life was centered on the Gospel, on the life of Jesus, on the smallest details of Jesus' earthly life.

So he went to Nazareth, once the theater of Christ's "hidden life." There he reverenced the presence not only of his Jesus, but also of Mary His Mother, and Joseph, the humble carpenter Jesus had chosen for His foster father.

We follow Francis now with greater awe to Bethlehem, the town where Christ was born. To Francis' eyes, this was indeed the world capital of "poverty." For Jesus, the Son of God, had chosen to be born there in a stable, and to receive the homage of poor shepherds and wealthy kings alike.

It would be a priceless treasure to know the thoughts, feelings, and inspirations Francis experienced in this most blessed of earthly places. Was it here perhaps that he was first inspired to reproduce the Crèche of Bethlehem, as he would later do at Greccio, thus making the first Christmas crib in all of Christendom?

But our pilgrim must have felt even stronger emotions at the sites of Christ's sufferings than either at Nazareth or Bethlehem. We can picture him kneeling on the hill of Golgotha, praying at the Holy Sepulcher, meditating at the very places where the world was redeemed through the sufferings of the Divine Master.

The vision of Christ's sufferings was to grow on Francis, and we have a proof in his stigmatization on Mount Alverna.

Four years were to elapse between Francis' pilgrimage to the Holy Places and that day in September, 1224, when the wounds of Christ would be imprinted into the Poverello's limbs. Was there not a link between the two events? We are left to our own conjectures about this matter, however, for the saint's early biographers say nothing about it. But since Francis' visit to Palestine is clearly established, the rest follows quite logically.

Return to Italy

Francis might have remained longer in the Middle East and renewed his efforts to preach to the infidels, had he not received news from Italy that obliged him to return without delay.

What was going on?

A special messenger sent by his friends brought him word that his lifework, that is to say, his Order, was threatened by all sorts of upheavals. This situation was the more serious because it was being caused by Francis' own representatives, that is, those he had left to oversee the brothers when he departed for the Middle East. We need not be surprised, therefore, to learn that the messenger, a lay brother named Stephen, had not been sent by the superiors but brought him news from a number of the other brothers.

To understand what was really happening, we must remember this was the year 1220. As we have seen in the preceding chapter, at that time the only Rule was the very simple one of 1210. The Order had since grown unbelievably fast. Young men had come by the thousands to be taught in Francis' spiritual ways. They were filled with good will, but totally inexperienced.

Before leaving, Francis had entrusted his powers — probably at the Chapter of 1219 — to Brothers Gregory of Naples and Matthew of Narni. But another chapter had now been held in which the superiors, with the approval of the older brothers in the Order, established stricter fasts, no doubt on the model of the ancient Orders such as the Cistercians. In their inexperienced hands the primitive Rule had become too austere for an Order of preachers of the Gospel. Until then, it seems the Minors had observed only the fasts imposed throughout the Church, adding the Wednesday fast. Fasting on Monday and Saturday was optional.

We do not know precisely what innovations were introduced during Francis' absence, but we know through our most reliable sources that when Brother Stephen reached Francis and his companion, Peter Catani, they were eating their meal and there was meat on the table. Now this was precisely one of the days when, according to the new regulations, there was to be fasting and abstinence from meat. After Stephen had delivered his message, Francis cast a glance at the platter of meat that had just been served, and said:

"Sir Peter" (he always called him "Sir" out of respect for his great learning) "Sir Peter, what shall we do with this?"

"Well," answered Peter Catani, "Sir Francis, we'll do whatever you deem best, for you're the only one who has the right to give orders."

"In that case," said Francis, "let's obey the holy Gospel and eat what has been served us!"

But Brother Stephen was bringing other news, calculated to greatly disturb Francis. In his absence, Brother Philip, who had been designated the Visitor to the Poor Clares, had gone to Rome to request the penalty of excommunication for anyone who would cause any harm to the nuns. Worse still, Brother John di Capella had gathered a number of discontented brothers like himself in an attempt to form a new Order, and had even initiated steps at the Roman Curia to obtain approbation for his plans.

All this bad news could not but fill Francis with indignation. His most faithful disciples had fallen into dissension and had not been ashamed to attack the institutions he had established. They had even had the gall to challenge the Holy See, as if the Order, verbally approved by Pope Innocent III in 1210, were escheated and abandoned. These were things he could not accept.

And how could he restore order among his followers? Obviously, there was only one way: by his presence.

When Francis learned all this bad news he had with him at St. John of Acre some of the most knowledgeable brothers of his Order: Peter Catani, Elias of Cortona, Caesar of Speyer, and a few others.

They must have held a quick conference and decided unanimously to return in all haste to Italy.

They took the first boat for Venice. In those days, the journey from Palestine to Venice took about a month. As soon as Francis and his brothers returned to Portiuncula, peace was quickly restored in the Order, as they had anticipated. The regulations established in his absence were annulled. But the need of writing a more precise and complete Rule had now become evident. We have seen in the preceding chapter how Francis decided to devote himself to this urgent task. That is why he delegated his governing powers to Peter Catani. Brother Peter was to be the Minister General until his death a few months later. After Peter Catani, Elias of Cortona was given the title of Vicar General by Francis. And we know that Elias, urged and counseled by Cardinal Hugolino, was not satisfied with the Rule of 1221. He wrote the Rule of 1223, which was to be approved on November 29th of that year by Pope Honorius III.

In the meantime, another important development took place. Francis created the memorable institution that was to be called the Franciscan Third Order. We shall learn more about it in the next chapter.

THE FRANCISCAN THIRD ORDER

By Geraldine K. Hollman,
member of the Franciscan Third Order

As Christians, we are all called to
follow Christ, or as St. Paul said:
"The life I live now is not my own;
Christ is living in me" (Gal. 2:20);
but there are many roads that one
may follow. One has the road sign:
Third Order of St. Francis. Just
what is a Third Order? What is
the Franciscan Third Order? How
did it come into being?

The canonical definition of a Third
Order has been given in Canon 685
of the Code of Canon Law: "It is
an association of the faithful who
make the profession to strive toward
Christian perfection, in a manner
suited to the secular life, by observ-
ing a Rule approved by the Holy See,
under the direction and according to
the spirit of a religious Order."
This definition would apply to any
Third Order; therefore, the key words
for us are "...according to the spirit
of a religious Order." How does an

Order, any Order, derive its spirit? The spirit comes from its founder. For the Franciscan Third Order it was the "Mirror of Christ," Francis of Assisi. Francis of Assisi — the shining light of the thirteenth century — who is as contemporary today as he was then. The poor little man of Assisi who turned his back on wealth, prestige, family and friends, security and, with a heart brimming over with love, chose instead poverty, ridicule, a whole new family of Poor Brothers, Poor Sisters and Penitents and found true security by embracing Christ Crucified.

When Francis first began to live the Gospel life, it gave him such freedom, such joy, such purpose in his life that it was quickly apparent to those who watched him and asked "why" that he had found "the pearl of great price," and slowly but surely Francis found himself with followers. This was to be the First Order. But there was also living in Assisi, another soul full of love for Christ and an unfulfilled yearning for truth — Clare. After consulting with Francis, she undertook to live the same Gospel life with her own sister and aunt, and we have the beginning of the Second Order, the Poor Clares.

But not all that saw the beautiful, crystal clear truth of Francis' way of living the Gospel could follow him into the religious life — not all had that calling; some had dependent parents, or other family obligations. But follow Francis they must. Or, in the words of his great biographer Celano "...a number of people, nobles and peasants, clerics and laymen, were moved by divine inspiration to come to St. Francis, desirous of placing themselves permanently under his care and direction. The Saint of God, as a stream flowing full with heavenly graces, poured out on all these the waters of God's blessings and carpeted the fields of their hearts with blossoms of virtue. He was their excellent artisan according to whose pattern, rule and teaching, since they were acclaimed so widely, the Church of Christ has been renewed in both sexes, and as a result the triple army of the elect marches triumphantly forward. And for all the faithful, likewise, he furnished a norm to live by and unerringly mapped out the way of salvation for them in their various stations of life."

Yes, Francis saw the need and filled it. Thus the Third Order of St. Francis came into being and for the sake of historical clarity the year 1221 is considered to be the year of the founding of the Order —the Third Order, not third in importance, not third in dedication, but simply third by reason of historical founding. As one recent Franciscan document says: "The Third Order should be greatly respected, effectively promoted, and considered necessary for the fullness of the Franciscan charism since it has its own proper mission in the Church and the world."

Unfortunately, we do not have a copy of this original Third Order Rule, but we do know that it was simple, drawing upon the actual words of the Gospel in much the same way as he did for the Rule for the Friars Minor and Poor Clares. We can reconstruct the content of Francis' original Third Order Rule by trimming away the many local customs added to very old editions that we do have. Or, the same spirit can be found in "The Letter to all Christians," which is extant. This letter called for the complying with all commandments and counsels of the Church, for the restitution of any ill-gotten goods, for fasting and penance, for the reception of Holy Communion more frequently than once a year (as set forth by the Lateran Council of 1215), for the practice of charity and obedience to lawful authority —in short, to follow "in the footsteps of Jesus Christ."

It is also known that Francis' original Rule was put into a more legal form by his friend and supporter, Cardinal Hugolino, shortly after this.

The Order of Penitents (original name) was open to secular priests and laymen — single and married, male and female, rich and poor — all God's people. The members of this Order therefore remained in the world without being of the world, rejecting the materialism of that day. This Rule — more specific than "The Letter to all Christians" — required the following: abstinence from meat on Mondays, Wednesdays, Fridays and Saturdays; certain prescribed periods of fasting; the recitation of the Divine Office, for those who could read; or the saying of fifty-four Our Fathers and Glory Be's for those who could not. There was a common fund to aid their needy members, certain prayers to be said for both the living and deceased members; the sick and destitute were visited regularly; great works of charity were performed; the making of a will was mandatory within a very short time of profession; and, as members of an Order, they were subject to the Church court rather than the secular court. Tertiaries were to avoid taking oaths except when necessary (remember, these were feudal times), and they could not bear arms except to defend right and justice. They wore distinctive clothing at all times, which was both modest and poor in appearance. The present Rule is very similar to this, with the exception of those items no longer applicable due to changes made by subsequent Popes and Vatican II.

We do not know exactly who was the first lay member, but tradition tells us that a wealthy merchant in the town of Poggibonsi by the name of Luchesio came to Francis after hearing him preach and asked for advice on his spiritual life. Francis told him that both he and his wife should follow a rule based on true Gospel living and it is believed that this rule was the Rule of the Order of Penitents. Immediately after this, Luchesio sold all his possessions, gave the money to the poor and both he and his wife adopted the Third Order habit, spending the rest of their lives giving witness to the Franciscan way of life in works of mercy.

The example of Luchesio and Buona Donna and other lay followers of Francis caused many to question their own good but empty lives, and Francis' way of life began to spread like wildfire. Almost everywhere in the little Italian towns and cities, particularly the places where Francis himself appeared and preached, similar groups came into existence.

It may be quickly surmised that the Third Order not only affected the spiritual lives of those undertaking this reform of their whole way of living in the world, but because of its very nature, affected the political and social life of all coming in contact with it. Some viewed it as a threat and it didn't take long for its members to be harrassed and even persecuted from many sides. The Popes were repeatedly called upon to defend the way of life of the Third Order of St. Francis and many did so. For example, in 1319 John XXII issued a bull defending the Third Order and recommending the Tertiaries to all prelates of the Church.

It should be pointed out, that the Third Order was, from its founding, lay administered. Its members were counseled to seek spiritual direction from the Order of Friars Minor, but the Third Order was self-governing. In the fourteenth and fifteenth centuries, the emphasis in Third Order living swung to more of a religious state and some, seeking even more of a commitment, undertook to live under vows in the religious life. Today we know them as the great Franciscan teaching orders, nursing orders, etc. The Third Order religious naturally felt a strong kinship to the secular branch of the Third Order, and felt it their duty and responsibility to have jurisdiction over it. Naturally over the years this presented many problems. So many, in fact, that in 1428 Martin IV issued a bull, *Licet inter cetera*, putting the Third Order under the jurisdiction of the First Order.

The Renaissance and the persecutions of the Reformation brought about a sharp decline in membership in the Third Order throughout all Europe but by the middle of the sixteenth century, the Third Order enjoyed an upswing in membership and began to show remarkable growth.

In the seventeenth and eighteenth centuries, the Third Order continued to make progress throughout the world. But in the latter part of the eighteenth century and the first part of the nineteenth century, the Third Order underwent its greatest decline and was almost wiped out. The major contributors to this decline were Emperor Joseph in Austria and the French Revolution.

In 1883 Pope Leo XIII revised the Third Order Rule, adapting it to the then modern times, but keeping its nature and spirit. Once and for all he settled the jurisdictional question by declaring, "...the Visitors are to be chosen from the First Franciscan Order or from the Third Order Regular." Pope Leo himself was a member of the Third Order and recommended the Third Order to the whole Catholic Church in the encyclical *Auspicato* and the constitution *Misericors Dei Filus.*

It can easily be seen that many Popes of the Church have not only been in favor of the Third Order of St. Francis as a way of life but have gone out of their way to become members and to promote it to the whole Church. The Holy See has repeatedly declared that the Third Order is a true Order. In *Tertium Franciscalium,* Pope Pius X declared, "The order (Third Order Secular) does not differ from the other two (The First Order and Second Order of St. Francis) in nature, but only insofar as it pursues the same purpose in a way peculiar to itself."

In more modern times Pope Pius XII stated, "The Third Order was born in the mind of your Seraphic Father the day that a group of souls, moved and urged on by his words, asked to be allowed to accompany him on the path he was traveling, following in the footsteps of Christ, in whose name he was constantly repeating the words, 'Be perfect' (Mt. 5:48). The Third Order of St. Francis was born to satisfy this thirst for heroism among those who, though having to remain in the world, did not wish to be of the world. The Third Order, then, seeks souls who long for perfection in their own state" (Address of July 1, 1956).

The Second Vatican Council has had a profound effect on the Third Order of St. Francis. Renewal efforts in the Third Order are producing great results, but this Franciscan family, ever loyal to the Holy See and its founder, Francis of Assisi, looks forward to the future and is ready to meet any challenge as it has in the past.

SAINT FRANCIS
AND NATURE

The sermon to the birds

Francis of Assisi had always
possessed certain qualities common
to the troubadours of his time. His
soul was so filled with love of God
that it thrilled with a poet's delight
over the beauty of all of God's
works. He was truly a friend of men,
but also a friend of nature and of
everything about it. He loved the
birds, the fish, the flowers, in a word,
everything that was alive, everything
that witnessed to God's infinite
wisdom.

We can safely say that this outlook on
nature was part and parcel of his
spirituality. While it focused on
penance, poverty, humility, on the
cross of the Savior, it was not gloomy
and sad, but, on the contrary, joyous
and outgoing. We need only call to
mind his dialogue with Brother Leo
on perfect joy. This was one of his
traits that had the greatest impact on
his contemporaries and attracted the
greatest number of enthusiastic and
enchanted disciples.

It has been said of the first English Franciscans that whenever they got together or even met in passing they couldn't keep from laughing. And if they laughed so heartily, it was not to scoff at the credulity of the common people. Their laughter was an explosion of inner joy, the joy of being God's creatures, whom God had so loved that He had sent His only Son to them.

Franciscan joy has remained a major element of the *Poverello's* heritage. We shall see how it found expression in unusual sermons and hymns of rare beauty.

One thing that had never yet been seen in the world, for example, was a sermon preached to birds. And yet the troubadour of Assisi performed this unique feat.

It was probably in the year 1212. Francis had undertaken a great mission campaign through Italy. Crowds gathered wherever he went. Even his brothers seemed frightened by the enthusiastic welcome he received everywhere, and especially when they heard the heady words: "Here comes the saint!"

Francis had reacted the best way he knew, sometimes by trying to appear ridiculous in the eyes of his admirers when he passed through towns, and again by humiliating himself in some way. But nothing made any difference. He finally began to wonder if he should not withdraw to a hermitage and renounce his life and work among men. It was then that Brother Masseo, whom he had sent to Brother Silvester and to Sister Clare for guidance, came back with their categorical answers: "God has not called you for your own sake alone, but for the salvation of all!"

"Well then," he said to Brother Masseo, "let's be on our way!"

They soon came to a place somewhere between Brevagna and Cannara.

According to our sources, notably the *Fioretti*, which agree with Celano:

"Here Francis saw a few trees by the side of the road. In these trees were thousands of birds of every species, such as no one had ever seen before. There were also many birds beneath the trees, in the fields. As soon as Francis saw this multitude, the spirit of God descended upon him and he said to the two disciples with him: 'Wait for me a moment. I'm going to preach to our brothers the birds!' Then he went into the field, and walked toward the birds on the ground. As soon as he began to speak, the birds in the trees flew down toward him, and stood around him not moving a feather, although they were so closely packed that some of them brushed against him...

"And Francis said to the birds: 'My very dear brothers the birds, you are deeply indebted to God, and it is your duty to praise Him and celebrate Him always and everywhere, for He has allowed you to fly freely wherever you please; He has clothed you with double or triple coats and given you elegant, many-colored finery. And you must also give thanks to the Creator for this food He gives you with no effort on your part. And then there is the beautiful voice He has given you to sing with! You neither sow nor reap, my dear little brothers, but God Himself feeds you, and it is He who gives you the brooks to quench your thirst, the mountains, hills, rocks, and woods to shelter you, and high trees where you can build your nests. And although you cannot spin or weave, He gives you and your little ones all the clothing you need. That's because the Creator loves you very much, as He has proven by so many great favors He has bestowed on you! But you, my dear brothers the birds, take care not to be ungrateful toward Him, and always busy yourselves praising Him.'"

This is a typically Franciscan sermon. Whatever Francis said to the birds, he also said in one form or another to the children of men. And there was nothing more "evangelical" than such a sermon. Since the time Christ walked on earth no one had heard such simple and yet profound appeals.

But the most extraordinary aspect of this unprecedented sermon to the birds, is that the birds themselves seem to have understood it very well.

The text continues: "And after Francis had spoken these words, all these little birds began to open their beaks, flap their wings, stretch their necks and bow their little heads to the ground in deep respect, and to show by their songs and their movements that they were truly delighted with what Francis had said to them. And the saint, for his part, was filled with joy at this sight, and wondered at this great multitude of birds, at their variety and diversity, as well as their great tameness. Then he praised the Creator for them, and gently, fraternally, urged them to join him in praising God.

"And when St. Francis had finished his sermon and his exhortation to praise God, he made the sign of the cross over these birds. They immediately flew away, singing with wonderful power and beauty. And soon they dispersed in every direction."

This first episode clearly reveals our Brother Francis' great love of nature as it speaks to us of God, reveals the goodness of God, and raises the thoughts of men toward God.

Francis commands the swallows

It was probably soon after the sermon to the birds that Francis and his companions arrived at Alviano, where his words had such a powerful impact that everybody in the town wanted to become his disciple. As we remember, this was one of the places where the future Third Order first sprang into being.

But we have also noted that another remarkable incident had made a strong impression on people's minds and added to the effectiveness of Francis' preaching. This was the incident of the "swallows," that has been related by Celano, St. Bonaventure, and also with certain variations in the *Fioretti*.

It was evening. Francis arrived with Brother Masseo at the principal square of Alviano, and began to preach. But the place was filled with countless swallows that had built their nests in the town's high walls and towers. They would flit to and fro with noisy chirps from their nests to the edge of the roofs, and back again. They made such a stir that humans could hardly hear themselves talk. Francis and Masseo, as was their custom, began to sing a Latin hymn to attract the townspeople. And they came in throngs. They were all standing there silent and motionless, waiting for Francis to preach, as his reputation for holiness had spread throughout the area.

Only the swallows persisted in their chirping marathon. Instead of quieting down, they seemed to delight in making as much noise as possible, and they kept coming in ever greater numbers to perch around the saint. He almost despaired of being heard.

Then an extraordinary thing happened. Francis turned to the chattering birds and said to them in the gentlest of tones, which seemed to penetrate everyone present: "My sisters, the swallows, I think it's my turn to talk now! You have done enough singing and chatting. Come now and listen to God's word, and be still and silent while I preach!"

The swallows immediately fell silent and remained where they were until the end of the sermon. We can understand that the witnesses to the scene were stupefied at the authority Francis wielded over the birds. Jesus had once commanded the wind and the storm on the Lake of Tiberias, and they had obeyed. He had also often commanded those possessed by devils, and delivered them. The swallows' obedience to Francis is a fact of the same order. The sanctity and presence of God within Francis worked miracles that restored to man the primacy over nature lost through original sin.

Other examples

Our sources are replete with similar incidents concerning the life and activities of Francis. He often cited the example of his "brothers" the birds to teach humans lessons in trust, and he did this especially for those who wanted to become his disciples. Jesus had done the same!

When he wanted to teach the religion of poverty, he would say, for example:

"Do the larks need more than a swallow of water from a spring and the food they find in the fields, before taking off into the sky to sing the Lord's praises so joyously, that everybody feels compelled to stop work and look skyward?"

Or again, talking about a species of Italian lark, commonly known as the "hooded lark," he said to his brothers: "Our sister lark has a hood, just as we do! It's a humble bird, as we can see, because it always goes to the side of the road to try to find a grain of corn. Its feathers are the color of the earth, and serve as models to teach us that we must not wear handsome, expensive, and gaudy clothes, but poor and simple clothes. And when it flies up into the sky, our sister lark praises God in a delightful way, as all the brothers of the Order should!"

The sense of universal brotherhood

One thing that seems to stand out in the citations we have just given is the insistence with which Francis talked about his "brothers the birds," and his "sisters the swallows" or the larks. He felt he had brothers and sisters throughout nature. As he saw it, all creatures had the same Father, and thus were all relatives in some ineffable way.

But let us understand our saint's thinking. For him everything is sacred because everything comes from God and speaks of God. It never entered his mind to confuse nature with God, or to identify himself with creatures not endowed with the capacity to think and to love.

There was not a trace of pantheism in his thinking. He remained faithful to the Catholic Church, which holds pantheism to be the most serious kind of heresy. Nor did he have any desire to lose himself in nature, as has happened to certain modern poets. Conversely, he was far removed from any belief in the insensibility of nature, the inevitability of fate, or the uselessness of prayer and hope in God. Everything about him spoke of faith, hope, and love. And he saw everywhere in nature proofs of God's generosity, God's teaching, and of the calls of His infinite love.

He found perfect expression of his sentiments in the first words of the Catholic Creed: "I believe in God, the Father almighty, Creator of heaven and earth!" Since God created all things, everything must bear the imprint of God, everything must talk to us of Him, everything must draw us toward Him. And when we feel we are surrounded by nature in all its beauty, we feel as though immersed in God's own love.

This is how we must understand Francis' love of nature. We find a most exquisite expression of it in his famous *Canticle of Brother Sun,* one of his finest legacies to posterity.

How "The Canticle of Brother Sun" was written

We come now to the latter days of Francis' life. While his spirit was still very much alive, its material wrappings were fast wearing out. His poor body was beginning to look more like a cadaver than anything else. The brothers used to whisper to one another that they would soon be losing him. His "crusade" in Egypt and his stay in Palestine had left him with an eye ailment that he had never wanted to have medically treated, saying that in illness one should humbly submit to God's will and remain joyful. This is why he preferred to retire into solitude, to be more totally immersed in God, his only love. So he went to St. Damian's, to the delight of Sister Clare, who quickly had a hut of branches built for him.

This was the summer of 1225. Francis had only one year to live. The sunlight at Assisi was so strong that he had to keep his eyes almost completely closed, and was practically blind for a time. Besides, he was subjected in his wretched hut to an unbelievable invasion of field rats or field mice that brazenly ran everywhere, even over his face, allowing him no rest night or day.

Despite these conditions his heart was so overflowing with the joy he had so often preached to his brothers that he was inspired to write his *Canticle of Brother Sun.*

The source of Francis' inspiration, as we know, was largely biblical. There was a precedent that had been particularly dear to the first Christians: "The Canticle of the Three Children in the Furnace." The Roman Breviary had placed this Canticle at the end

of Lauds for Sunday, a canticle of thanksgiving by
all creatures:

> "Sun and moon, bless the Lord;
>   praise and exalt him above all forever.
> Stars of heaven, bless the Lord;
>   praise and exalt him above all forever.
> Every shower and dew, bless the Lord;
>   praise and exalt him above all forever.
> All you winds, bless the Lord;
>   praise and exalt him above all forever.
> Fire and heat, bless the Lord;
>   praise and exalt him above all forever.
> Cold and chill, bless the Lord....
> Light and darkness, bless the Lord..."
>
> > (Dn. 3:62-67, 72).

And similar hymns of praise could be found in
the Psalms as well. Francis had been nourished by
all these prayers. He had spent his whole life since
his conversion praising God. We should not be surprised, therefore, to see him concentrate on universal
praise in his poor hut close to the monastery of his
daughters at St. Damian's. For it was here he had
made his first steps in the exclusive love of his
Jesus and of poverty. Now his poet-saint's heart
yearned to sing out his praise.

It was when he could no longer see any of
nature's beauty because daylight hurt his poor, sick
eyes, that he burst into words of joy and enthusiasm
for the works of his God.

"The Canticle of Brother Sun"

In his hut at St. Damian's, Francis' sufferings
were sometimes so cruel that the following anguished
prayer was torn from his heart: "Lord, come and help
me, that I may patiently endure my sickness!"

And he immediately heard God's answer deep within his soul. A voice said to him: "Tell me, Brother, wouldn't you be very happy if, in exchange for the pain you now suffer, you were given a treasure compared to which the whole earth would have no value?" And as Francis agreed, the voice continued: "Well then, Francis, rejoice and sing! Sing while you are there, weak and sick, for you are earning nothing less than the kingdom of heaven!"

The next day Francis got up very early and said to the brothers who were taking care of him: "If the emperor were to give me the whole empire as a gift, should I not be very happy about it? Well now, the Lord has just given me the heavenly kingdom, right here and now while I'm still alive here on earth. So in spite of all my trials, it is only right that I be filled with joy and thank God the Father, Son, and Holy Spirit. And that's why I want to compose for our consolation and the good of our neighbor, a new hymn of praise on the creatures of the Lord that we use every day and without which we would be absolutely unable to stay alive."

After this little discourse, he became recollected like someone deep in contemplation. But the very next instant the brothers heard him intone the first stanza of what we call *The Canticle of Brother Sun.*

Let us read this admirable Canticle attentively, as the most fervent of prayers. Like all great things, it is very, very simple.

It goes without saying that Francis was singing in Italian, even though he was very fond of the French language. And *The Canticle of Brother Sun* has been transmitted to us in Italian. We have translated it as literally as possible:

Most High, Almighty, good Lord,
To You be praise, glory, and honor, and all
    blessings;

To You alone! Most High, do they belong,
And no man is worthy of speaking Your name!
Be praised, Lord, with all Your creatures,
And above all our Brother Sun,
Who gives us the day by which You light
our way,
And who is beautiful, radiant, and with his
great splendor
Is a symbol to us of You, O Most High!
And be praised, Lord, for our Sister Moon and
the Stars,
You created them in the heavens, bright,
precious, and beautiful!
And be praised, Lord, for our Brother the Wind,
And for the air and the clouds, and for fair
weather and all other,
Through which You sustain Your creatures,
And be praised, Lord, for our Sister Water,
So useful, and humble, and chaste!
And be praised, my Lord, for our Brother Fire,
Through whom You light up the night,
And who is handsome, joyful, robust, and
strong!
And be praised, my Lord, for our Sister, Moth-
er Earth,
Who supports and carries us,
And produces the diverse fruits and colorful
flowers and the trees!
Praise and bless the Lord and give thanks
to Him
And serve Him with great humility!

Such was the initial text of *The Canticle of Brother Sun*, which might also be called *The Canticle of Creatures*. But the following year, when the doctor told Francis he would soon die, Francis cried out: "Well then, welcome my Sister Death!"

And as if the thought of leaving this earth had again kindled his poetic muse, he added this last stanza:

Be praised, my Lord, for our Sister, bodily
    Death,
From whom no living man can escape!
Woe only to those who die in mortal sin;
But blessed are those who have done Your most
    holy will;
For the second death can cause them no harm!

And so *The Canticle of Creatures* was finished.
The welcome to "our Sister Death" brought it to
completion. For Francis, everything was a source of
joy, because everything comes from God and leads
to God, who is Joy and Love!

THE CRÈCHE AT GRECCIO, THE STIGMATA, THE DEATH OF FRANCIS

Christmas, 1223

Among the events of the last years
of Francis' life, there is one we have
not yet mentioned that occurred
shortly before the writing of *The
Canticle of Brother Sun.* We shall
simply call it "the Crèche of
Greccio."

To understand it, we must remember that Francis, like other Christians
but no doubt more than most,
had a special love and tender
devotion for the feast of Christmas.
This is truly the feast of gentleness,
humility, generosity, and above all
poverty. The Poverello's heart
melted with love at the thought of
the little Child born in a stable.
Very probably, his visit to Bethlehem
during his prolonged pilgrimage to
the Holy Land helped nourish and
increase these sentiments in his soul.

In 1223, he had the opportunity to
make another journey to Rome on the

occasion of the approbation of his Rule by Pope Honorius III. He was received by Cardinal Hugolino, but was soon disturbed by the honors and attentions with which he was surrounded, either at the Cardinal's residence or at the home of the noble and pious Roman lady whom he called "his Brother Jacqueline."

He therefore left Rome as fast as he could. On the way home, he saw once more his beloved Rieti valley, then stayed among his brothers of Fonte Colombo in the Sabine Mountains.

Close by lived a fine man named John Vellita who held Francis and his Order in high esteem. In fact, he had given them a rocky piece of ground planted with trees, facing the town of Greccio.

Shortly before the Christmas of 1223, Francis asked this man to come to see him at Fonte Colombo.

When Sir Vellita came, Francis said to him: "I should like to celebrate the holy night of Christmas with you; but listen to the idea that has come to me! In the woods close to our hermitage you will find a cave among the rocks. There you are to set up a manger filled with straw. And we also need an ox and an ass, just like at Bethlehem, because at least once in my life I want to celebrate the coming of the Son of God upon earth in a fitting way, and see with my own eyes how poor and miserable the One who was born for love of us chose to be!"

John eagerly entered into Francis' plans. He did everything as he had been told. During the holy night the brothers came from Fonte Colombo, and the inhabitants of the region, alerted to what was going on, came in throngs to attend this most unusual celebration of Christmas. They all carried lighted torches to find their way in the dark. Around the entrance to the cave, the brothers stood with their lighted candles. And so the night was filled with light. The whole wood was as bright as if it were noonday. The dark vault of the pines shone with unaccustomed brilliance.

A table had been placed above the manger for the Mass. Beneath this improvised altar lay the Infant God, between the ox and the ass. It was such a new and amazing sight that Sir Vellita thought he saw a real child in the Crèche, but he seemed to be either sleeping or dead. And then Francis came and took the Child in his arms. Suddenly the Child woke up, smiled at the Poverello, and caressed his cheeks and beard with his little hands. Was this a dream, a vision? Sir Vellita could not tell.

One thing he did know was that Francis' preaching had worked this miracle now unfolding before his eyes. Francis had brought to life the Child God whom so many Christians seemed to have forgotten.

After the Gospel for the Midnight Mass had been sung, Francis, in deacon's vestments, stood next to the altar. Celano, his first biographer, recounts this scene to us. He says: "Francis sighed deeply, and seemed to be brimming over with wonderful joy." In his strong, pleasant voice, he preached on the love of the Supreme Good.

We can only wish we had the exact text of this sermon. Francis was not just an eloquent speaker. It could be said of him, as of Jesus: "No one has spoken like this man!" He spoke less with words than with his heart, which seemed to beat in each of his words and gestures. As one of his biographers has said: "His words were filled with sweetness. He spoke of the poor King who deigned to be born on this night, of the Lord Jesus in the city of David. And each time he came to the name of Jesus in his sermon, he seemed to glow with love, and instead of pronouncing the name, he would say 'the Child of Bethlehem.' And he uttered the word 'Bethlehem' with the voice of a little bleating lamb; and after he had said it he would run his tongue over his lips as if to savor the sweetness this name left on his lips as it passed. And the holy festivities did not end until very late, when everyone finally returned home with joyful hearts.

"And later on, this place where the manger had been placed was consecrated to the Lord and became a church, and above the grotto an altar was placed in honor of our blessed Father Francis. So, on this spot where once two animals devoid of reason ate the straw of the manger, henceforth men would come for the salvation of their souls and bodies, to receive the immaculate Lamb, our Lord Jesus Christ, who in His ineffable love gave His blood for the life of the world, and who lives and reigns with the Father and the Holy Spirit in eternal power, world without end. Amen."

Let us add that Greccio is still a mecca for pilgrims, and that the feast of Christmas is the scene of great manifestations of devotion even today.

The saint's illnesses

The feast of Christmas, 1223, was one of Francis' last great joys. From that time on, his joys would come only from his sufferings. He was approaching the blessed end of his life. And yet he was still a relatively young man. Born in 1182, he had just reached his forty-first year in 1223. Admittedly, he had paid little attention to his body, and his health had never been robust. In his youth, he had suffered several attacks of fever. After his conversion, he had undergone unbelievable privations, frequent and prolonged fasts. Sometimes he had had scruples about it and thought he heard the devil say to him: "All sinners can be saved, except those who have

destroyed themselves through excessive mortifica-
tions!"

If we examine his way of life closely, we find
it was not calculated to build up his health. He slept
very few hours a night, almost always sitting up or
with his head propped on a log or a rock for a pillow.
He rarely agreed to eat epicurean dishes, and if he
suspected they were too delicious he would pour
ashes over them, saying half-apologetically: "Our
Sister Ash is chaste!"

When he was alone at the Carceri, one of his
favorite hermitages on the slope of Mount Subasio
close to Assisi, or later on Mount Alverna, he would
always lie down on the cold, bare earth, or more
precisely, on the bare rock. All this was obviously bad
for his health. In less than twenty years he had ruined
his body. He had hemorrhages that caused a great loss
of blood. On several occasions it seemed as though
he would die of one. Besides, his journey in the
Middle East had left him almost blind.

Indeed, this inspired preacher was now almost
too weak to speak in public. He had strength only
to pray, to meditate, and to weep.

And yet it was during this last period of his
life that he composed a number of letters that have
been preserved, as well as his *Testament* and *The
Canticle of Brother Sun*, which we have just admired
as his swan song.

Last writings

We have five letters written by Francis during
this last period of his life: *The Letter to All Chris-
tians; The Letter to the Chapter of Pentecost, 1224;
The Letter to All Ecclesiastics; The Letter to All
Guardians* (or superiors of the brothers); and *The
Letter to All Authorities.*

Most critics agree that there is nothing new in these letters. Francis did not seek to make a brilliant showing in them. He simply said what he had always said, and did not write any high-sounding phrases. And so these letters are in a sense dull and monotonous. But if we remember they were written by a soul on fire, that they were the last effort of a great friend of Christ Jesus, we cannot fail to read them with great devotion.

What did he say? What we already know: that we must love and serve God; that we must live a life of conversion, penance, and abstinence in every sense of the word—that is to say, both moral and spiritual; that we must love our enemies and come to their assistance, not seek temporal learning or high position; that we must pray much, confess our sins regularly and receive Communion; and finally, that we must do the best we can to repair all the evil we have committed.

In his *Letter to All Guardians* or superiors, he spoke of the specific duties of the brothers, of respect for the Blessed Sacrament, for all writings containing sacred words, for the divine services, and concern for the immaculate cleanliness of sanctuaries, churches and sacred vessels.

The fact that he also wrote a *Letter to All Authorities* is proof of Francis' sense of social awareness. He realized that God had called him to influence his times. In fact, he addressed himself in the name of our Lord "to all the Podestas, Consuls, Magistrates, and Rectors." And he invited them all to give good example to those under their rule by receiving the sacraments of the Church regularly. And he declared they would be making wise use of their authority if, through a herald or some other means, they reminded their people that they must all pray and praise God.

Is it possible this thought came to him after seeing the muezzins call the Moslems to prayer? It is quite likely that the practice of reciting the *Angelus*, which was to become very widespread a little later, had its origin in our saint's admonition to the public authorities. Less than forty years after his death, in 1263, the General Chapter of Pisa called for the recitation of the *Hail Mary* when the church bells rang at dusk.

These letters were written with care, and it is possible Brother Caesar of Speyer helped Francis to compose them, as his secretary. But there was also a humbler, simpler, more intimate and touching letter, the *Letter to Brother Leo*, which we reproduce in its entirety:

"Brother Leo, greetings and peace from your Brother Francis! I say to you, my Son, in truth and as though I were a mother, that all the words we spoke on our journey can be summed up in this advice: in whatever way you think it is right for you to please God, walk in His footsteps, and follow His poverty, do it with the blessing of God and my permission! And if you find it necessary to consult me later on, either for the salvation of your soul or for some other consolation, and you want to come to me, then come!"

The original of this letter, a precious relic, has been preserved in the cathedral of Spoleto since 1902.

At Mount Alverna

We must now follow Francis to Mount Alverna, where great things were about to happen.

As we remember, this mountain had been given to our saint by a young lord, and Francis had sent two brothers to take possession of it. With the help of the devout donor, Count Roland, these two brothers had established themselves on a rocky plateau at the top of the mountain. There they had constructed a few huts made of branches and mud, such as Francis favored. Later on Count Roland had a small church built there, which was given the same name as the one at Portiuncula: Our Lady of the Angels.

During the summer of 1224, Francis' health seemed to improve. He decided to go to Mount Alverna to celebrate the great feast of the Assumption. Afterwards, he intended to fast for forty days in preparation for the feast of St. Michael, which fell on September 29.

Several of his most faithful brothers accompanied him on this last expedition. Naturally there was Leo, and also Angelo, Masseo, Silvester, and Illuminato.

It was a long, hard journey for Francis up the mountain from the valley of Rieti. Several times his strength gave out. The brothers then asked a peasant to let them have the use of his donkey for their Father. The peasant came up to Francis with his donkey and naively asked him:

"Are you the Brother Francis that everybody is talking about?"

Francis said he was indeed.

"In that case," the man answered, "you'd better make sure you are as good as people say you are, because many have put their trust in you!"

Francis was so moved by this appeal to goodness that he got on his knees and kissed the peasant's feet.

The same man probably served as a guide for the brothers, leading the donkey bearing Francis to the top of Alverna. It is recounted that on the ascent the guide became terribly thirsty, and Francis began to pray that his thirst might be relieved. He then told the peasant of a spring close by, which they had not known about, where he could quench his thirst.

The *Fioretti* relates a charming story about this journey toward Mount Alverna, which brings out once again Francis' close kinship with all of God's creatures.

On their way up, the brothers stopped for a moment to rest under an oak tree, and a great flock of birds flew into their midst. There were joyful bird cries and the flapping of wings. Better still, several birds came and perched on Francis' head, others on his shoulders, showing that they had really come on his account. Birds even came on his knees and into his hands. And Francis saw this as a delicate favor from his God.

"My dear brothers," he said, "I really think it pleases our Lord Jesus Christ that we should come and stay on this solitary mountain, because the birds are so happy to see us!"

When Count Roland heard about Francis' arrival with his brothers, he came with a large escort, bringing bread and wine and other provisions for the brothers. He found the entire Franciscan community at prayer. Afterward Francis went to greet the Count, and they had a long talk. Francis expressed his gratitude to the Count and asked him to have a little hut built under a magnificent beech tree, just a stone's throw from the brothers' huts. He felt he would be well situated there to carry on his contemplation in solitude. His wish was granted without delay. That evening, Francis gave a sermon to the brothers and the Count's entourage. Before Count Roland left, he begged the brothers to ask him for whatever they would need during their stay at Alverna.

Francis then told his brothers the rule he wanted them to follow. "Above all," he said, "let us preserve holy poverty. Let us beware of ever abusing

such generous offers as the Count has just made."
And he concluded with these memorable words:
"As I see I shall soon die, I have resolved to spend
much time alone with God, so I can repent of my
sins. Brother Leo may bring me a little bread and
water when he feels like it. But if anyone comes
you must answer in my place, and make sure you don't
let anyone through to me!"

Then he blessed them and retired to his hut,
while the brothers went to theirs.

Francis' sufferings

All the early texts concerning the last days of
Francis discreetly suggest that he was filled with
anxiety about his life's work. What was to become of
his Order? It was as if his whole life had been a
dream. He had begun alone. He remembered his
joy at the very beginning, in the caves around Assisi.
But everything had developed so fast. God had sent
him brothers. The first little group of twelve disciples had grown by leaps and bounds. A great Order
had come into being. He had given its direction to
Brother Elias of Cortona. But now he heard that
Brother Elias was unveiling plans, formulating
ambitions, and granting dispensations within the
Order which seemed contrary to what he, Francis,
had intended.

Actually the whole of Christendom was in a
state of intellectual revolution. Universities were
coming into existence on every side. Many of the
lesser brothers felt the need to take part in the movement. They were collecting books and burying
themselves in study and in hot pursuit of higher
learning! What would this mean for the holy poverty
Francis was constantly holding up to them? Some of
Francis' faithful companions had even been heard

to say, with Brother Giles: "Paris! Paris! You are leading our brothers to ruin!"

In the solitude of Alverna, all these things whirled about in Francis' mind. He wanted to make order out of this chaos. And so he turned to the Gospel, as he had always done, to find an answer. He commanded Brother Leo to open the sacred book, probably the missal, three times. And each time, Leo opened to a page concerning our Lord's Passion. Francis understood that God was telling him he was to devote the rest of his life to the contemplation of his Savior's cross.

The stigmata

During this time, the feast of the Assumption was celebrated. Francis spent it with his brothers, but afterwards he stayed apart from them even more than before. He chose an isolated spot, at the bottom of a rocky gorge. To reach it, one had to cross over on a large tree trunk flung over the canyon. Only Brother Leo was allowed to come to Francis twice a day, but he had to ask permission to approach each time. One evening Leo didn't hear Francis answer him as had been arranged. Daring neither to go back nor come forward, Leo stood for a long while, not knowing what to do. Then in his concern, he tried to catch a glimpse of his master, and saw him deep in prayer. He even heard what Francis was saying: "My beloved Lord and Master, what am I in comparison with You: a miserable earthworm, a poor, useless servant!"

But even the slight sound Brother Leo made aroused Francis from his prayer. He asked who was there. More dead than alive, Leo answered: "It's I, Leo!" And Francis very gently complained that he had disobeyed. But he soon forgave him, and even told him the meaning of his meditations. He finished with these words: "This is the meaning of these words that you have heard, little lamb of God! But in the future take care not to spy on me, and now return to your cell with the blessing of God."

The days passed, and soon it was September 14, the feast of the Exaltation of the Holy Cross. On the morning of that feast, Francis prayed with extended arms, his face turned toward the east. And this was his prayer:

"O Lord Jesus Christ, there are two things I shall ask of You before I die! First, that I may experience in my soul and in my body the sufferings You endured, O sweet Jesus, in Your passion! And second, that I may, insofar as possible, feel in my body the boundless love that You, the Son of God, felt and which impelled You to want to suffer so many tribulations for all of us miserable sinners!"

And it seemed to Francis that his prayer was already answered. He began to burn with a consuming love and felt as though completely changed and *transformed into his Jesus.*

Our source, which is very ancient, goes on to say: "And while he was thus on his knees, he saw a seraph descend toward him, with six gleaming wings. And this seraph came very close to him, so that he could see very distinctly that he bore the image of a crucified man. His wings were disposed in the following manner: two wings rose above his head, two others were outspread in readiness to fly, and the two others covered his entire body.

"When Francis saw this, he was filled with fright, joy, and sorrow. He felt great joy at seeing that his Jesus deigned to show Himself to him and cast a glance of such great tenderness toward him. But he was deeply grieved to see his Jesus crucified. And he was filled with wonder over such an amazing apparition.

"It disappeared very slowly, but left in Francis' heart the flame of an immense love. And from that

instant the apparition also left miraculous marks of
Christ's sufferings in his very limbs. For there
immediately began to appear in his hands and feet
traces, as it were, of nails...."

And likewise, on the saint's right side, the
image of the lance thrust appeared in the form of a
bloody, red scar. And drops of blood would often
flow from these miraculous wounds, wetting Francis'
tunic and pants.

"He refused to tell the brothers anything
about these wonderful things, but on the contrary
strove constantly to keep them hidden. But when
the brothers washed his clothing they understood
their master did indeed bear in his side, in his hands
and feet, the bodily image and likeness of the wounds
of our Lord Jesus Christ!"

This miracle of stigmatization has recurred
many times in other persons, but apparently never
in such a pure, perfect, and eloquent manner as in
Francis himself.

Supernatural joy

The first fruit of the miracle of the stigmata
seems to have been a truly supernatural joy, which
Francis expressed in a "Laud" or "Praise" that Brother Leo preserved for us. Here it is in translation:

"You are holy, Lord God, You are the God
above all gods! You alone are the author of miracles.

"You are strong, You are great, You are the
Most High!

"You are the Almighty, You are the Father most
holy and King of heaven and earth.

"You are the Triune and the One, Lord God
above all the gods!

"You are the all-kind, the all-merciful, the
supreme God, the living and true God!

"You are love, You are wisdom, You are humility, You are patience!

"You are beauty, You are certitude, You are peace and joy!

"You are our hope, You are justice and measure, You are our riches!

"You are gentleness, You are our protector, You are our defender and our safeguard!

"You are our refuge and our strength!

"You are our faith, our hope, and our love! You are the great sweetness of our souls!

"You are the infinite Good, the great and wonderful Lord, almighty, all-merciful, all-compassionate, and our Savior!..."

On September 30, 1224, Francis left Mount Alverna on a donkey Count Roland had provided, because now he couldn't walk any more. Before setting out for Portiuncula, he said good-bye for the last time to Alverna with great emotion: "Farewell, farewell, farewell, to everyone and everything here! Adieu, holy mountain; adieu, Mount Alverna; adieu, mountain of the angels! Adieu, my dear Brother Falcon who used to awaken me with your cry; I thank you for your solicitude for me! Adieu, great rock where I used to pray: I'll never see you again! Farewell, Church of St. Mary! And farewell, Mary, Mother of the eternal Word; I entrust to your care the sons I leave here!"

Then he set out for Assisi with Brother Leo, passing through villages where he was received with acclaim. On his return to Portiuncula, he felt so well he thought he would be able to resume his missions as before, but this was only a false recovery. He was living on borrowed time.

We have already told how he came, exhausted and sick, to rest at St. Damian's, and how he wrote his *Canticle of Brother Sun* there in the summer of 1225.

As winter winds began to blow, he was at the hermitage of San Eleuterio, and it is possible he spent the last Christmas of his life at Fonte Colombo and at Greccio.

The last months

The last months of Francis' life were a long preface to death. He became visibly weaker from day to day. He was now held in such high esteem in the Church that Pope Honorius III, who had been obliged to leave Rome as the result of an outbreak of violence and was now living at Rieti, sent his own physicians to take care of Francis. They tried out on his poor body all the methods of the barbaric therapeutics of that time: bloodletting, plasters, vesicants (agents that induced blistering), and so on. And as none of these measures were of any help, they turned to heroic methods: the application of ignipunctures on both the dying man's temples!

Francis cried out: "My Brother Fire, I know you are nobler and more useful than most other creatures! But you know, too, that I've always been kind to you and always shall be, out of love for the One who created you! Well then, won't you be gentle and kind to me and not burn me more than I can endure?"

Then the torture by fire began. When the brothers smelled the burned flesh, they fled in horror. But when it was all over, Francis merely said: "If that isn't burned enough, you can do it again, because I didn't feel any pain at all."

The medical treatment given Francis at Rieti did not improve his condition. From there Francis had the brothers take him to Siena, renowned for its excellent air. But he didn't get any better there either. One night after he had experienced a brief respite, he suffered such violent hemorrhages that the brothers thought surely he was dying. They knelt by his bed to ask for a final blessing. Francis asked his confessor, Brother Benedict of Prato, to bring a pen and some ink, and then said: "Write down that I bless all my brothers, all those who are in the Order and all who will enter it until the end of the world! And as a sign of this benediction that I give them, and in remembrance of me, I leave them this Testament: namely, that they must always love one another, as I have loved them and still love them; that they must all love and honor our holy mistress, Lady Poverty; and that they must always faithfully obey the prelates and priests of the holy Church."

Toward Assisi

But the end was not yet. Francis soon expressed the desire to see his beloved Assisi once more. Brother Elias, who was governing the Order, commanded that he be taken there. But he feared that the sick man, whom everyone considered a saint and already, as it were, a "relic," might be waylaid en route. So he sent him to Assisi by all sorts of detours. Finally after great hardships, the convoy reached Assisi. Francis had the joy of bringing about a reconciliation between the Podesta and the Bishop, who were at loggerheads. He had now added what is called "the stanza of forgiveness" to his *Canticle of Brother Sun:*

"Be blessed, Lord, for all who, for Your sake, forgive their enemies,

"And have to suffer injustice and tribulation;

"And blessed are those who persevere in peace,

"For they will be rewarded by You, Most High!"

When the Podesta heard this stanza, he was so deeply moved that he threw himself at the Bishop's feet and asked his forgiveness, while the Bishop in his turn confessed he had been too harsh and kissed the Podesta with affection.

Very soon afterward, Francis composed the stanza to "my Sister Death," which we have already quoted.

One of the most beautiful things he did toward the end was to dictate his *Testament,* an admirable document in which he reviewed his life, recalled his conversion, his first kiss to the leper, his love for churches, which he wanted to repair and rebuild, and the great desire God had implanted in his heart to live the Gospel integrally. He gave his brothers his final recommendations: obedience to their superiors and to the holy Rule, poverty, and the daily recitation of the Divine Office, concluding with these words:

"And the brothers must not say that I am giving them a new Rule, for this is only a lesson, an admonition, an encouragement. It is simply the Testament that I, your little Brother Francis, leave you, my Brothers, so that you may observe the Rule in a more perfect and more Catholic way, because all of us have sworn to the Lord that we would follow it."

The end

Francis also had the consolation of being taken to Portiuncula. And when they passed by the leper hospital that held so many memories for him, he had the brothers halt the litter. He raised himself up a little from his stretcher, looked out for the last time over Assisi with its border of mountains on one side and valleys on the other. Then he slowly lifted his hand in a supreme gesture of love and traced the sign of the cross over the city of his birth, saying: "May the Lord bless you, for He has chosen you to be the home of those who acknowledge Him and glorify Him in truth and want to honor His name!"

Very soon after that, at Portiuncula, Sister Death came to reunite him with his God. Among his last consolations was a visit from his "Brother Jacqueline," who had rushed to his side from Rome when she learned of his impending death. He had the holy Gospel read to him for the last time, the text being about the washing of feet at the Last Supper; *The Canticle of Brother Sun* was sung to him once more, and throughout the singing the dying Francis' lips kept repeating the last verse of the Canticle: *"Be blessed, Lord my God, for our Sister Death!"*

And now it was Saturday, October third. The doctor came and Francis asked him when the gates of eternal life would open for him. He also insisted that the brothers pour ashes over him. "For," he said, "soon I shall be nothing but dust and ashes."

Toward evening he began to sing Psalm 142: "With a loud voice I cry out to the Lord; with a loud voice I beseech the Lord...."

He had time to sing the Psalm all the way through, including the last verse:

"Lead me forth from prison, that I may give thanks to your name. The just shall gather around me when you have been good to me."

His prayer was answered. He entered eternity singing. What a magnificent end for God's troubadour!

The funeral of the man everyone considered a saint was a veritable triumph. The funeral procession made a stop at St. Damian's, where Clare and her sisters gave the highest homage to their dearly beloved Father.

Few men have had such a profound and beneficent influence on their own century, and on all succeeding ages within the Church. Why? Those of our readers who have stayed with us will readily understand our answer: *Because he loved so much!* In his heart burned the fire that Jesus had come to cast upon the earth and without which the earth is only a valley of tears and darkness.

On the Feast of St. Joseph
L. Cristiani
FRANCISCAN TERTIARY

Daughters of St. Paul

MASSACHUSETTS
 50 St. Paul's Ave., Jamaica Plain, Boston, MA 02130; **617-522-8911.**
 172 Tremont Street, Boston, MA 02111; **617-426-5464; 617-426-4230.**
NEW YORK
 78 Fort Place, Staten Island, NY 10301; **718-447-5071; 718-447-5086.**
 59 East 43rd Street, New York, NY 10017; **212-986-7580.**
 625 East 187th Street, Bronx, NY 10458; **212-584-0440.**
 525 Main Street, Buffalo, NY 14203; **716-847-6044.**
NEW JERSEY
 Hudson Mall—Route 440 and Communipaw Ave.,
  Jersey City, NJ 07304; **201-433-7740.**
CONNECTICUT
 202 Fairfield Ave., Bridgeport, CT 06604; **203-335-9913.**
OHIO
 2105 Ontario Street (at Prospect Ave.), Cleveland, OH 44115;
  216-621-9427.
 616 Walnut Street, Cincinnati, OH 45202; **513-421-5733; 513-721-5059.**
PENNSYLVANIA
 1719 Chestnut Street, Philadelphia, PA 19103; **215-568-2638.**
VIRGINIA
 1025 King Street, Alexandria, VA 22314; **703-683-1741; 703-549-3806.**
SOUTH CAROLINA
 243 King Street, Charleston, SC 29401; **803-577-0175.**
FLORIDA
 2700 Biscayne Blvd., Miami, FL 33137; **305-573-1618; 305-573-1624.**
LOUISIANA
 4403 Veterans Memorial Blvd., Metairie, LA 70006; **504-887-7631;
  504-887-0113.**
 423 Main Street, Baton Rouge, LA 70802; **504-343-4057; 504-381-9485.**
MISSOURI
 1001 Pine Street (at North 10th), St. Louis, MO 63101; **314-621-0346;
  314-231-1034.**
ILLINOIS
 172 North Michigan Ave., Chicago, IL 60601; **312-346-4228; 312-346-3240.**
TEXAS
 114 Main Plaza, San Antonio, TX 78205; **512-224-8101; 512-224-0938.**
CALIFORNIA
 1570 Fifth Ave. (at Cedar St.), San Diego, CA 92101; **619-232-1442.**
 46 Geary Street, San Francisco, CA 94108; **415-781-5180.**
WASHINGTON
 2301 Second Ave., Seattle, WA 98121; **206-441-3300**
HAWAII
 1143 Bishop Street, Honolulu, HI 96813; **808-521-2731.**
ALASKA
 750 West 5th Ave., Anchorage, AK 99501; **907-272-8183.**

CANADA
 3022 Dufferin Street, Toronto 395, Ontario, Canada.